Behold
I Do
A New Thing

Behold
I Do
A New Thing

Morayo Isi

"Behold I will do a new thing; now it shall spring forth; shall ye not know it? I will make even a way in the wilderness, and rivers in the desert." Isaiah 43:19.

ISBN 978-0-9854740-2-7

Published by: Royal House Ministries

P. O. Box 420756,

Houston, TX 77242

Telephone number: 281-965-6727

Email: royalhouseministries@gmail.com

Printed in the United States of America

The Lord gave the word: great was the company of those that published it.
Psalm 68:10-12

Special Dedication

This book is dedicated to the person of The Holy Spirit, who is the GREATEST Author of all ages. Not only is HE my BEST friend and CLOSEST ally but He is my STRONGEST critic. He teaches me what and how to write and then goes the extra mile and helps me to perfect it.

To GOD alone be glory and praise forever. Thank You my darling Holy Spirit. You are EXTRAORDINARY!!!

May You continue to reign in my life, my home, my ministry, my writing……..

CONTENTS

CONTENTS

iv

INTRODUCTION

"Behold, I will do a new thing; now it shall spring forth; shall ye not know it? I will even make a way in the wilderness, and rivers in the desert." Isaiah 43:19.

"Remember the former things of old: for I am God, and there is none else; I am God, and there is none like me, Declaring the end from the beginning, and from ancient times the things that are not yet done, saying, My counsel shall stand, and I will do all my pleasure: Calling a ravenous bird from the east, the man that executeth my counsel from a far country: yea, I have spoken it, I will also bring it to pass; I have purposed it, I will also do it." Isaiah 46:9-11.

Please sing this prayer chorus with me from the bottom of your heart:

Do something new in my life
Something new in my life
Do something new in my life today
Do something new in my life
Something new in my life
Do something new in my life today

I cannot do it without you
I cannot do it without you
I cannot do it without you today
I cannot do it without you
I cannot do it without you
I cannot do it without you today.

Today, as you start this book with this powerful prayer song, I want you to be very specific in talking to the Lord. In what area of your life do you need a change, a new thing to manifest speedily? As you sing the song above, just tell the Lord the new thing that you want Him to do for you. Please be very specific. Cry to Him now in your own words, in your own way, in your own language.

Now that you have done that, your expectations shall not be cut off in Jesus name. Your new things shall spring forth speedily in the name of Jesus. Receive the answer to your prayers in Jesus name.

The Lord God does a new thing when He advertises His power and His glory in and through a person's life. He springs forth new things in various areas of life such as marriage, career, ministry, academics, business, and health.

God does new things in different ways. He can open up the heavens over various areas of your life and release the dew of heaven over them and cause them to blossom like they have never done before. He can make impossible situations to become possible or make a way where there is no way. He can turn a person's point of mockery into his point of laughter and joy. God can show up when your Lazarus has been dead and buried for four days and is already stinking and then turn the dead situation into a testimony that all eyes can see. He can throw new doors open for you to walk through that have never before been opened to anyone in your family or even your generation before. You then become a history maker and a nation shaker when He uses you to rewrite the history of your family, nation, and even continent.

To accomplish this, He might relocate or reposition a person. He can give a new name or a new organ to replace a bad one. He can ordain a new time and season, a new walk, fresh fire, new vision. He can initiate a new project, a new relationship, or new connections. He can also give new grounds and territory to make up for all the stagnant or wasted years. He can take a person to new heights. He can replace your spiritual eyes so that you can see the new things that He is putting together for you. He can change your garments and give you one that will no longer hinder your movement so that accelerate your progress.

Are you standing in line for a miracle? As you read this book and get connected to the God that does new things, obstacles will give way and new things will spring forth in every area of your life in the name of Jesus. Receive your new things now in Jesus name.

Behold
I Do
A New Thing

CHAPTER 1

BEHOLD, I DO A NEW THING

"Forget the former things; do not dwell on the past. See, I am doing a new thing! Now it springs up; do you not perceive it? I am making a way in the wilderness and streams in the wasteland." Isaiah 43:18-19.

"Behold, the former things are come to pass, and new things do I declare: before they spring forth I tell you of them." Isaiah 42:9.

"Therefore if any man be in Christ, he is a new creature: old things are passed away; behold, all things are become new." 2 Corinthians 5:17.

WHAT IS A NEW THING?

A new thing means different things to different people depending on your particular circumstances. For the sick, a new thing could be healing. For the lonely and abandoned it could be a new and fulfilling relationship. For a poor and hungry man, it would be financial breakthrough or even food. Even if you are already wealthy, a new thing could usher in even more wealth and honor than before. It could bring good health. For the captive or the oppressed, a new thing is freedom because as he is expectant, Jesus, the yoke breaker, comes in, breaks all the fetters and sets him free.

"The Spirit of the Lord is upon me, because he hath anointed me to preach the gospel to the poor; he hath sent me to heal the brokenhearted, to preach deliverance to the captives, and recovering of sight to the blind, to set at liberty them that are bruised." Luke 4:18.

Let us now look at the various meanings of a "new thing."

1

Change

"All the days of my appointed time will I wait, till my change come."
Job 14:14.

A new thing indicates that change has come. It means that the old paradigms or models are shifting. It indicates that there is an existing situation which is no longer acceptable or good enough hence the need for a new thing. It is the introduction of a better thing than was previously available.

For the new thing to manifest, the old thing has to give way. The status quo has to change. Doors have to be closed on certain things so that new doors can open for better things to come in. If you hold on to your old way of doing things that have not worked in the past, you will keep getting the same result as before such as failure, mediocrity, slow progress, stagnancy, retrogression, and other undesirable things.

A new thing therefore indicates that stagnancy and non-achievement have come to an end and that your life is moving forward.

New Season

"To everything there is a season, and a time to every purpose under heaven." Ecclesiastes 3:1.

A new thing indicates that it is a new season. It is a new phase or level in a person's life. A new thing is when your season of mourning turns to dancing and you get beauty for ashes. **Isaiah 61:3.** It is when the joy of the morning replaces the dark and long nights with its loneliness and tears.

It is what is described in the Bible verse below:

"Thy light break forth as the morning, and thine health shall spring forth speedily: and thy righteousness shall go before thee; the glory of the LORD shall be thy reward." Isaiah 58:6-10.

Pray like this:
O Lord, ordain a new time and season in my life now, in the name of Jesus.

New Glory

In the word of God we learn that it is possible to grow from glory to glory. **2 Corinthians 3:18.** Some people's glories have been vandalized in one way or the other. Such glories may have been exchanged, destroyed, buried, or hidden. God does a new thing when He cuts off the evil hands manipulating your glory so that it can manifest and shine. He does a new thing when He removes the evil veil that is covering your glory and potentials so that you can arise and to shine.

"Then shall thy light rise in obscurity, and thy darkness be as the noon day." Isaiah 58:6-10.

"The glory of the latter house shall be greater than the former." Haggai 2:9.

"Arise, shine; for thy light is come, and the glory of the Lord is risen upon thee. For, behold, the darkness shall cover the earth, and gross darkness the people: but the Lord shall arise upon thee, and his glory shall be seen upon thee." Isaiah 60:1-2.

A New Song and a New Dance

"And he hath put a new song in my mouth, even praise unto our God: many shall see it, and fear and shall trust in the Lord. (Psalm 40:3).

God does a new thing when He does the extraordinary and the miraculous in your life. As the scripture above says, when this happens, all eyes including those of your enemies that thought that it would never happen get to see it. The wonder of it all causes a new song to spring forth in your mouth like it did in the lives of Hannah, Mary, Moses, and David in the Bible. You then join the song writer in singing unto the Lord the following song:

> **I am singing a new song today**
> **I am singing a new song today oh**
> **What my father cannot do**
> **Jesus did it in my life**
> **I am singing a new song today**

It is when God does the unusual and you are so overjoyed about what the Lord has done that you dance a new dance to your new song as Miriam, Moses' sister, did in the Bible in **Exodus 15:20:**

> **I am dancing a new dance today**
> **I am dancing a new dance today oh**
> **What my father cannot do**
> **Jesus did it in my life**
> **I am dancing a new dance today.**

A New Name

"And the Gentiles shall see thy righteousness, and all kings thy glory: *and thou shalt be called by a new name,* **which the mouth of the LORD shall name." Isaiah 62:2.**

"He that hath an ear, let him hear what the Spirit saith unto the churches; To him that overcometh will I give to eat of the hidden manna, and will give him a white stone, *and in the stone a new name written,* **which no man knoweth saving he that receiveth it." Revelation 2:17.**

God does a new thing when He gives you a new name. Names are very important to God. We see that God Himself named several important personalities in the Bible including Our Lord Jesus who was named "Jesus" and "Emmanuel". **Luke 1:31, Isaiah 7:14.** Others are John the Baptist, King Josiah, Abraham, and Sarah. **Luke 1:13, 1 Kings 13:2, Genesis 17:5, 15.**

Getting a new name is one of the benefits of redemption. You take on the name of Jesus which is the most powerful name in this world and in the world to come. The Bible talking about the uniqueness and greatness of that name, writes that God, in the name of Jesus, has given us a name that is above every other name. This name "Jesus" carries such an awesome anointing that at the mention of it, every knee must bow and every tongue confess that Jesus is Lord. **Philippians 2:9.** This makes the name "Jesus" a very powerful weapon in the hand of a believer to disgrace the enemy.

There is power in the name that you bear. This can be either for good or for evil. Some people in the Bible bore bad names and it impacted their destinies negatively. Such names include Jacob, which meant "trickster;"

4

Jabez, which meant "I bare him with sorrow;" and Ichabod, which meant "The glory has departed."

Some names are bad because they glorify the devil and not God. They do not edify. An example of such a name is Linda which means serpent. Another is the African name meaning "Doctor." "Doctor" here simply refers to a sorcerer and witch doctor. Evil names attract hardship, problems, and bad luck to the life of the bearer. They keep bondages, stubborn yokes, hardship, and oppression in place. If you or your family bear such names, please prayerfully change it. You do not have to live under the cloud of an evil name. Jesus died to give you a new name in Him, so there is no reason for you to retain a name that is depreciating and altering your destiny.

God changed several people's names in the Bible to enable them to fulfill their God given destinies. He changed Jacob's name from "trickster" to "Israel" which means "One that prevails with God and man." Abraham and Sarah's names were changed from "Abram" and "Sarai," to align their lives to God's vision of making them the parents of nations. **Genesis 17:5, 16.**

Today, you too should find out the meaning of your name. If it is bad then you should prayerfully ask God for a new name and then change it. Please do not allow sentiments to continue keeping you in bondage.

New Open Doors

"I know thy works: behold I have set before thee an open door, and no man can shut it: for thou hast a little strength, and has kept my work, and hast not denied my name." Revelation 3:8.

God is does a new thing when He opens fresh doors of opportunities for you to walk through. He can open doors that have been shut against your family for generations. **Isaiah 61:4.** These new doors take you to new realms in various areas of your life including marriage, career, education, business, and ministry.

New Revelation

"The secret things belong unto the Lord our God: but those things which are revealed belong unto us and to our children for ever." Deuteronomy 29:29.

When the Lord does a new thing you get fresh revelation. Revelation is a new word from the Lord. It will always put you at the right place at the right time. It relocates and repositions you for success. Revelation was what helped the early apostles and church leaders to set new records everywhere that the Holy Spirit led them. Everything that they did was by revelation.

"As they ministered to the Lord, and fasted, the Holy Ghost said, Separate me Barnabas and Saul for the work whereunto I have called them. And when they had fasted and prayed, and laid their hands on them, they sent away. So they, being sent forth by the Holy Ghost, departed unto Seleucia; and from thence they sailed to Cyprus." Acts13:2-4.

Our Lord Jesus was the same. Talking of walking in fresh revelation daily, He said that He only did what He saw His father do. **John 5:19-20.** In other words, He continually downloaded fresh revelation from His Father that enabled Him to do all the mighty works that He did.

New Life

"Ho, every one that thirsteth, come ye to the waters, and he that hath no money; come ye, buy, and eat; yea, come, buy wine and milk without money and without price. Wherefore do ye spend money for that which is not bread? and your labour for that which satisfieth not? hearken diligently unto me, and eat ye that which is good, and let your soul delight itself in fatness. Incline your ear, and come unto me: hear, and your soul shall live; *and I will make an everlasting covenant with you,* even the sure mercies of David." Isaiah 55:1-3.

Salvation brings forth new life. For a person that has been wallowing in sin and in darkness, it is a new thing to come out of such terrible darkness into the marvelous light of Christ Jesus.

"Therefore if any man be in Christ, he is a new creature: old things are past away; behold all things are become new." 2 Corinthians 5:17.

At salvation, a person's identity is changed in Christ. One then begins a new life walking in the newness of life. **Romans 6:4.** All that belongs to Christ now becomes ours by reason of our new birth and inheritance in God through Christ. What a glorious inheritance. All of Abraham's blessings now become ours by adoption through Christ. **Galatians 3:14.**

New Covenant

At redemption, we begin to operate under a new and better covenant written and sealed with the blood of Jesus. This gives us the power to break free from every evil covenant that previously held us bound with all its attached curses.

"Blotting out the handwriting of ordinances that was against us, which was contrary to us, and took it out of the way, nailing it to his cross." Colossians 2:14.

Ancestral covenants, marine and witchcraft covenants, familiar spirit covenants, occult covenants, evil soul tie covenants, and all other satanic covenants are shattered when we get saved and delivered.

To secure our total freedom, Lord Jesus has also made provision for any curse that may kick in when we consciously or unconsciously break the terms evil covenants that we are party to:

"Christ hath redeemed us from the curse of the law, being made a curse for us: for it is written, Cursed is every one that hangeth on a tree: That the blessing of Abraham might come on the Gentiles through Jesus Christ; that we might receive the promise of the Spirit through faith." Galatians 3:13-14.

7

New Fire

"John answered, saying unto them all, I indeed baptize you with water; but one mightier than I cometh, the latchet of whose shoes I am not worthy to unloose: he shall baptize you with the Holy Ghost and with fire." Luke 3:16.

"And there appeared unto them cloven tongues like as of fire, and it sat upon each of them. And they were all filled with the Holy Ghost, and began to speak with other tongues, as the Spirit gave them utterance." Acts 2:3-4.

God does a new thing when He baptizes us with fresh fire from the altar of the Almighty. This represents a fresh in filling of the Holy Ghost and His fire upon us. Ephesians 5:18. This is to enable us to do our divine assignment and fulfill our divine purpose. With this fresh fire, things that could not be accomplished before are done with ease. This is why Lord Jesus asked His followers to be filled with fire before working for Him. Acts 1:8.

New Wine and New Wine Skins

"And no man putteth new wine into old bottles; else the new wine will burst the bottles, and be spilled, and the bottles shall perish. But n wine must be put into new bottles; and both are preserved." Luke 5:37-38.

God does a new thing in our lives by replacing our old wine that has lost its flavor with new and fresh wine. The scripture above teaches that we should not put new wine in old wine bottles or both the new wine and the old wine bottles will be destroyed. The new wine is the new thing that God has birthed forth in your life. The old wine bottles should be replaced with new ones that can carry this new wine. The new wine bottle is the new structure that has to be put in place to sustain the new thing that God is doing in your life. This new structure includes a new foundation built on Christ Jesus, the only solid Rock on which anything can be successfully built. 1 Corinthians 3:11.

It also includes new attitudes, mind sets, spirit, new friends, and new ways of doing things. These changes are needed to sustain the new thing that God is doing or it will die.

New Garments

"No man putteth a piece of new cloth unto an old garment, for that which is put in to fill it up taketh from the garment, and the rent is made worse." Matthew 9:16.

Your spiritual garment, just like the physical garment that you were in the natural, is whatsoever you are wearing in the spiritual realm. You may be wearing good spiritual garments such as praise, thanksgiving, success, prosperity, glory, favor, honor, and joy. Conversely, you may be wearing evil garments such as nakedness, frustration, reproach, shame, sorrow, untimely death, disgrace, poverty, failure, laziness, confusion, and disfavor. Evil garments hinder, pollute, cover, and cage a person's destiny.

The Lord does a new thing in a person's life when evil garments are replaced with new and beautiful garments. Blind Bartimeus experienced this turnaround when his old beggarly and limiting garments were replaced with new garments and he received new eyes and was able to see. **Mark 10:49-50.**

PRAYERS
1. **Every garment of darkness upon my body, I tear you off and I set you on fire. Roast now.**
2. **Every power, spirit, and personality, sowing evil garments into any area of my life, fall down and die.**
3. **You evil garment prepared for me, you are not my size, therefore be roasted to ashes.**
4. **Holy Spirit, arise and change my garment to the best that You have for me.**

New Eyes and New Ears

"Where there is no vision, the people perish: but he that keepeth the law, happy is he." Proverbs 29:18.

The Lord equips you with new Holy Ghost glasses. You get a fresh vision. If you can see the vision of the new opportunities that are available to you the battle is half won. It makes it easier to take possession of. Your responsibility is to write the vision down and run with it.

"And the LORD answered me, and said, Write the vision, and make it plain upon tables, that he may run that readeth it." Habakkuk 2:1-3.

This new vision to a large extent will drive all the changes that are needed to bring about the new thing that God is doing in a person's life.

When God does a new thing, you also get new ears that get awakened every morning with the voice of the Holy Spirit bringing you fresh instructions for the day as it says below in **Isaiah 50:4.**

"The Lord GOD hath given me the tongue of the learned, that I should know how to speak a word in season to him that is weary: he wakeneth morning by morning, he wakeneth mine ear to hear as the learned."

New Tongues

"And these signs shall follow them that believe; In my name shall they cast out devils; they shall speak with new tongues." Mark 16:17.

To enable you to be able to sustain the new thing that God is doing in your life you are given a new tongue. This is the new tongue that Our Lord Jesus promised before His ascension, that the Holy Spirit would impact on believers. **Mark 16:17.** It is so important and pivotal to the new things that God wants to do in the life of a believer that Our Lord Jesus told His disciples to wait in Jerusalem and be filled with the Holy Spirit which is evidenced by speaking in this new tongue before attempting to do any of the work that He assigned to them before He left. **Acts 1:4-5.** The new tongue manifested in the book of Acts:

"And they were all filled with the Holy Ghost, and began to speak with other tongues, as the Spirit gave them utterance." Acts 2:4.

The new tongue is the evidence of being filled with the Holy Spirit. **Acts 2:3-12.** It is the only language that the devil and His agents cannot understand or intercept. It throws them into total confusion. By using your new tongue you are cooperating with God to bring about wonder new things in your life. It helps you to get closer to God and to get more of His power to accomplish His divine assignment and purpose for you on earth.

10

New Hands and Feet

Your hands are a symbol of your handiwork such as your career, business, ministry and education. Terrible things can happen to a person's hand in the spirit realm which then manifests in the physical as afflictions, hardship, and failure. Hands can be polluted, cursed, chained, tied up, cut off, exchanged, and carry evil load such as demonic cobwebs.

When God does a new thing, these afflicted hands are replaced with new hands which prosper in every good thing that they are laid upon to do. I prophesy over your life that this season the Lord is giving you brand new hands which will bring you prosperity in every area of your life including your career, business, marriage, ministry and education in Jesus name.

Your feet are a symbol of your establishment. They are also the symbol of your dominion, which is why the bible says that wherever the sole of your feet shall tread, God will give it to you. **Deuteronomy 11:24.** The Lord is giving you brand new feet that will establish and settle you in every area of your life in Jesus name. The old dirty and polluted feet are been replaced by the beautiful feet that carry the gospel. **Isaiah 52:7**. The injured feet, the crippled lame feet, and the amputated feet are also being replaced with new ones that will enable you to run the race that is set before you instead of being stagnant, crawling, or retrogressing. **Isaiah 52:7, Romans 10:15.** I decree over your life that today that every spirit of rising and falling comes to an end in the name of Jesus. Circular problems end today also.

PRAYERS

1. Every witchcraft vehicle and driver reversing my progress backwards, catch fire and be roasted to ashes.
2. Powers assigned to reposition me from the front to the back die.
3. I am the first, I shall not become the last in Jesus name.
4. I put upon my feet the supernatural shoes of our Lord Jesus Christ and I declare that I shall not fall or fail in the name of Jesus.
5. I am a success and not a failure in the name of Jesus.
6. Every ancestral strongman blocking my chances, fall down and die.
7. Every evil hand assigned to put pluck out my star, wither and be cut off by fire in the name of Jesus.
8. Power for a new beginning fall upon me now in Jesus name.

A New Spirit

"A new heart also will I give you, and a new spirit will I put within you: and I will take away the stony heart out of your flesh, and I will give you an heart of flesh. And I will put my spirit within you, and cause you to walk in my statutes, and ye shall keep my judgments, and do them." Ezekiel 36:26-27.

God is a spirit and those who worship Him must worship Him in spirit and in truth. **John 4:24**. We, therefore, need a new spirit to relate with God effectively as His children. When we open the door of our heart to God through salvation then the Father, the Son, and the Holy Spirit come to dwell in us. We become the temple of God, living altars that carry God and His Spirit everywhere that we go.

"Even the Spirit of truth; whom the world cannot receive, because it seeth him not, neither knoweth him: but ye know him; for he dwelleth with you, and shall be in you." John 14:16-18.

When we give our lives to Our Lord Jesus Christ, we become married to Him. He takes over our whole lives and His spirit comes to dwell in us. It is this spirit that makes you a new man that can now do all things through Christ. This spirit is like new wine because it changes everything in our lives starting from our very perspective on life.

"But ye are not in the flesh, but in the Spirit, if so be that the Spirit of God dwell in you. Now if any man have not the Spirit of Christ, he is none of his." Romans 8:9.

It is this new spirit that makes us believe that we can do all things through Christ. It is the spirit that helps us to walk with God and not conform to the world around us. It leaves no room for inferiority complex, lack of confidence, or failure.

New Heart

"A new heart also will I give you, and a new spirit will I put within you: and I will take away the stony heart out of your flesh, and I will give you an heart of flesh." Ezekiel 36:26.

God is very interested in the condition of our hearts. The Bible says that man looks at the outward appearance but God looks at the heart. **1 Samuel 16:7.** A new heart is talking about a circumcised heart. The old stony heart is replaced with a heart of flesh which is more pliable and totally yielded to the word of God and the Lordship of Our Lord Jesus Christ. **Ezekiel 11:19, Ezekiel 36:26, Hebrews 10:16.**

This new heart is committed to doing the will of God in every situation. **Romans 2:29.** It enables us to cede control of our lives totally to God. A new heart is only possible in a man by the Spirit of God:

"And because ye are sons, God hath sent forth the Spirit of his Son into your hearts, crying, Abba, Father." Galatians 4:5-7.

New Shoes

"Now this was the manner in former time in Israel concerning redeeming and concerning changing, for to confirm all things, a man plucked off his shoe, and gave it to his neighbor; and this was a testimony in Israel. Ruth 4:7.

New shoes signify change. This could be in various areas of life such as in your ministry, career, marriage, or business. The type of shoe normally indicates the kind of change that is coming. Are they career shoes, ministry shoes, marital shoes, or casual shoes?

New shoes also signify new authority and new strength to crush the powers of darkness.

"Thy shoes shall be iron and brass; and as thy days, so shall thy strength be." Deuteronomy 33:25.

"Behold, I give unto you power to tread on serpents and scorpions, and over all the power of the enemy: and nothing shall by any means hurt you." Luke 10:19.

New shoes often signify changes in the area of marriage. For example when a single person dreams that she went to the market and found a matching pair of shoes that she likes, then her marriage is at hand. Mismatched shoes on the other hand, indicate that she should not go ahead with that particular relationship. At the very least she needs to seek the face of God about it.

Are you walking with no shoes? To be bare footed in the dream indicates lack of preparedness, poverty, or lack of protection. It can also indicate marital problems and if care is not taken divorce.

New shoes also signify restoration.

"But the father said to his servants, Bring forth the best robe, and put it on him; and put a ring on his hand, and shoes on his feet" Luke 15:22.

The old worn out shoes are replaced with new shoes to enable you run with the new vision and new things that God is doing in your life.

New Choices

When the Lord does a new thing, new opportunities are opened up to us. We cannot seize all these opportunities at once because resources such as time and money are limited. This means that we have to prioritize, make choices, and take decisions.

God does not force the new things that He is doing in our lives on us. We are always allowed to be free will agents to make our own choices. This has been the case right from Adam and Eve. We can either choose to cooperate with God or to reject the new thing that He is offering us. For example, in a situation where God presents a couple to each other as His ordained partners for marriage, one could agree with God's choice and the other totally disagree. God will not force any of His intended partners. Yes, it is a God opened door but you can choose not to walk through that open door.

PRAYERS

1. Spirit of error and mistake, I am not your candidate, therefore die.
2. Power to make the right choices in life fall upon me in Jesus name.
3. I refuse to be manipulated out of God's blessings for my life.
4. I will not be cheated by the devil. I will extoll myself.
5. You the fake me, clear away, the original me, manifest now by fire.
6. I receive divine direction for my life by the power in the blood of Jesus.
7. Power to find my bearing in life, fall upon me now, in Jesus name.
8. O Lord, this is my year, this is my season of marriage therefore arise and give me my right match.
9. I refuse to make the wrong choices in life in the name of Jesus.
10. I refuse and reject every demonic manipulation and control in every area of my life, in the name of Jesus.
12. In my .... (career, marriage, ministry, business, education, etc) O God, arise and change my status in the name of Jesus.
13. O Lord, in my career, ministry, marriage, business, arise and replace my old worn out shoes with new ones.
14. If I am wearing the wrong shoes, O Lord, arise and put upon me my correct shoes.
15. I put upon my feet, the shoes of our Lord Jesus Christ, and I declare by the power in the blood of Jesus, that I shall not fail or fall in Jesus name.

CHAPTER 2

WHO IS DOING A NEW THING?

It is God that is doing a new thing. We believe that God can and does new things because He has the Final say in every situation. He is JEHOVAH!!! He is the Great I Am.

In every situation, God is the "I Am." Like He told Moses to tell His people, whatever you need God to be in your situation, today He can be that:

"Thus shalt thou say unto the children of Israel, I AM hath sent me unto you." Exodus 3:14.

If we need money, He becomes our provider. If we need healing He becomes, The Great Physician, our healer. When we need a father He is the Everlasting Father. And when we need a lover, He is the Lover of our Soul. When we need a helper, He is our Helper, The Helper of the Helpless, and The Ever Present Help in Trouble.

Since we believe that God will do new things in our lives, let us sing to Him again our prayer song for this book:

> **Do something new in my life**
> **Something new in my life**
> **Do something new in my life today**
> **Do something new in my life**
> **Something new in my life**
> **Do something new in my life today**

Now let us take an in-depth look at who our God really is. Doing this will convince us and leave us with no iota of doubt that our God can indeed do new things in our lives. In actual fact, He can do exceedingly, abundantly above all that we can ask, think, or imagine. **Ephesians 3:20.** We are also told that eyes have not seen, no ears have heard, neither has it even come into the heart of any man the new things that God wants to do for us that love Him. **1 Corinthians 2:9.** Do you love the Lord? Then you are a candidate for new things. Receive them in Jesus name.

He is the faithful God

"God is not a man, that he should lie; neither the son of man, that he should repent: hath he said, and shall he not do it? or hath he spoken, and shall he not make it good?" Numbers 23:19.

"Shall I bring to the birth, and not cause to bring forth? saith the LORD: shall I cause to bring forth, and shut the womb? saith thy God." Isaiah 66:9.

God will do new things in our lives because He keeps His word. He cannot lie. Everything He has promised to do in His word, we can hold Him to and He will perform them in our lives.

"For as the rain cometh down, and the snow from heaven, and returns not thither, but waters the earth, and makes it bring forth and bud, that it may give seed to the sower, and bread to the eater. So shall my word be that goes forth out of my mouth: it shall accomplish that which I please, and it shall prosper in the thing whereto I sent it." Isaiah 55:10-11.

He is the Sovereign God

"Declaring the end from the beginning, and from ancient times the things that are not yet done, saying, My counsel shall stand, and I will do all my pleasure" Isaiah 46:10.

God said that He would have mercy on whoever He chooses to have mercy. **Roman 9:15, 18.** God is sovereign and has the final say in every situation. If you believe that, please sing this chorus with me:

I say who has the final say?
Jehovah has the final say
I say who has the final say?
Jehovah has the final say
Jehovah turns my life around
Jehovah turns my life around
He makes a way
Where there seems no way
Jehovah has the final say

17

God is Limitless

"For my thoughts are not your thoughts, neither my ways your ways, saith the Lord. For as the heavens are higher than the earth, so are my ways higher than your ways and my thoughts higher than your thoughts." Isaiah 55:8-9.

Human beings are limited by their experiences, environment, foundation, genes and other factors. But God is limitless hence the Bible tells us that all power belongs to God. **Psalm 62:11.** He can do anything that He chooses with it. Our Lord Jesus confirmed this saying:

"And Jesus came and spake unto them, saying, All power is given unto me in heaven and in earth" Matthew 28:18.

So we should not try to limit God in our lives because His ways are much higher than ours. He is the Ancient of Days that transcends time. He is the Alpha and Omega, without beginning and without ending. He was there before the foundation of the world. He alone knows the end of a thing from the beginning.

He is the Rewarder

God rewards all who diligently seek Him **Hebrew 11:6.** We see this all over the Bible. He told father Abraham that He was his great reward. **Genesis 15:1.** He told the children of Israel that He did not ask them to serve Him in vain:

"I have not spoken in secret, in a dark place of the earth: I said not unto the seed of Jacob, Seek ye me in vain: I the Lord speak righteousness, I declare things that are right." Isaiah 45:19.

He teaches His children how to profit. **Deuteronomy 8:18.** He also gives them power to get wealth. **Isaiah 48:17.** All these benefits are for us through Christ. We should key into them.

He is the Unchangeable God

"For I am the Lord, I change not; therefore ye sons of Jacob are not consumed." Malachi 3:6.

God is the unchangeable changer. God's attributes and character remain unchanged but just a touch from Him and people's lives are changed forever. So we see that God never changes even though His mighty works in our lives do change daily hence it is written:

"Jesus Christ the same yesterday, and today, and forever." Hebrew 13:8.

He is the Miracle Working God

He is the God that makes impossibilities possible. **Isaiah 45:2-7.** Nothing is too difficult for Him. **Jeremiah 32:17.** He is the miracle working God. He is invisible but His great works are so visible in our lives. He brings honey out of the rock. Today He will turn every lack in your life to abundance. He moved Joseph from the prison to the palace in just twenty four hours and promoted him from prisoner to Prime Minister. Not only that the Bible records that Joseph became a father to Pharaoh. **Genesis 45:8.** What a marvelous God. He can make the miraculous to become the norm for you also if you will let Him.

He is the Covenant Keeping God

"As for me, this is my covenant with them, saith the LORD; My spirit that is upon thee, and my words which I have put in thy mouth, shall not depart out of thy mouth, nor out of the mouth of thy seed, nor out of the mouth of thy seed's seed, saith the LORD, from henceforth and forever." Isaiah 59:21.

God is the covenant keeping God, who keeps His own end of any bargain that He makes with man. We must take God at His word because a promise from God is guaranteed. Once God has spoken, a contract kicks in. Contracts between God and men are sealed with the blood of Jesus. All that He requires is that we do our part. He always does His part.

"My covenant will I not break, nor alter the thing that is gone out of my mouth." Psalm 89: 34.

He is the Door Opener (Psalm 24)

He is the One that opens new doors for you and no man can shut them.

"I know thy works: behold, I have set before thee an open door, and no man can shut it: for thou hast a little strength, and hast kept my word, and hast not denied my name." Revelation 3:8

"And the key of the house of David will I lay upon his shoulder; so he shall open, and none shall shut; and he shall shut, and none shall open." Isaiah 22:22.

In other words, when God says yes to your breakthroughs, no power, spirit, or personality can say no.

My Father Open the Door of Joy for Me

1. My father, open fresh doors of opportunity for me in every area of my life, in the name of Jesus.
2. O Lord, open miracle doors for me now, in the name of Jesus.
3. You the door of ...., (specify the door you want God to open for you) be lifted up and open wide for me now.
4. O Lord, do not allow the enemy to turn my open door of joy into sorrow and tears, in the name of Jesus.
5. O Lord, let sorrow and tears be far away from me and my home.
6. Every power that has tied me up, making me unavailable for blessings, release me and die now, in the name of Jesus.
7. My Father, open doors of breakthroughs for me that the enemy cannot close in the name of Jesus.
8. My enemies will not turn my open doors of blessing and fulfillment into sorrow and weeping in Jesus name.
9. Any power assigned to close my open doors of opportunities, die.
10. Rivers in high places that will make me great, open by fire.
11. I am that I am, arise and manifest your power in my life.
12. Thank you Lord for opening new doors for me.

CHAPTER 3

WHERE DOES GOD DO THE NEW THING?

"But upon Mount Zion shall be deliverance and there shall be holiness; and the house of Jacob shall possess their possession." Obadiah 1:17.

New things spring forth after deliverance. Deliverance takes place on Mount Zion, the Mountain of the living God. **Obadiah 1:17.** It is where God tabernacles and is allowed to express Himself in the lives of His people. This is where His spirit dwells and where His spirit is, there is liberty. **2 Corinthians 3:17.** It is where His word is taught and exemplified without compromise. It is where God's presence is and where His power is available to break yokes and set the captives free continuously. This is well described in the following scriptures:

"Thou hast ascended on high, thou hast led captivity captive: thou hast received gifts for men; yea, for the rebellious also, that the Lord God might dwell among them. Blessed be the Lord, who daily loadeth us with benefits, even the God of our salvation." Psalm 68:18-19.

New things spring forth in the place of prayer and fasting. They spring forth in the place of worship. They break forth on the mountain of holiness and on the altar of consecration and brokenness.

PRAYERS
1. Place your right hand on your head and say: Fire of deliverance fall upon my life.
2. O God, arise and destroy the powers behind my problems.
3. Powers assigned to pull me down, die now, in the name of Jesus.
4. O God, arise by all the power by which you are known as God and command deliverance upon my life.

CHAPTER 4

HOW DOES GOD DO A NEW THING?

God is sovereign and cannot be put in box as Uzzah learnt to his own destruction. **2 Samuel 6:1-7.** God can do new things anyway He chooses including new ways that have never even come to the heart of man. **Ephesians 3:20, 1 Corinthians 2:9.** Let us now examine some of the ways that He goes about doing this.

By Remembering You

Let us take this chorus together:

> **Remember me o Lord**
> **Remember me o Lord**
> **Remember me o Lord today**
> **Remember me o Lord**
> **Remember me o Lord**
> **Remember me o Lord today**

God does a new thing by remembering you and solving your problems for you. God remembered Hannah, the mother of Prophet Samuel, and she who had been barren for a long time conceived and had Samuel:

"And Elkanah knew his wife; and he LORD remembered her. Wherefore it came to pass when the time was come about after Hannah had conceived that she bare a son and called his name Samuel saying, because I asked him of the LORD" 1 Samuel 1:19-20.

God remembered the children of Israel and took them out of 400 years of bondage in Egypt and brought them into Canaan Land, the land of promise. **Exodus 6:5.** He will remember you and do the same for you today, in Jesus name.

By Opening the Heavens

God does a new thing by opening up the heavens over various areas of a person's life and flooding them with blessing. This is particularly true where the heavens have become brass with no rain falling to bring good things. God controls the windows and doors of Heaven. **Malachi 3:10.** Open heavens ends the dryness and allows showers of blessings to pour from heaven unimpeded. After the heavens opened as Jesus was being baptized in the River Jordan, His life and ministry changed dramatically. **Matthew 3:16.**

By Taking Away Reproach

God does a new thing, by taking away whatever is causing reproach in our lives. This is what He did for Rachel, the wife of Jacob. He remembered her after years of barrenness and took away her reproach by giving her a son with a glorious destiny, Joseph:

"And God remembered Rachel, and God hearkened to her, and opened her womb. And she conceived, and bare a son; and said, God hath taken away my reproach." Genesis 30:22-23.

He did the same for Zacharias the old priest and his wife Elisabeth, by giving them a son, John the Baptist, whom our Lord Jesus referred to as the greatest of all the Old Testament prophets:

"And in those days his wife Elisabeth conceived, and hid herself five months, saying: Thus hath the Lord dealt with me in the days wherein he looked on me, to take away my reproach among men." Luke 1:24-25.

By Bringing an End to Rejection

"To the praise of the glory of his grace, wherein he hath made us accepted in the beloved." Ephesians 1:5-7.

God does a new thing by bringing an end to the history of rejection, disappointment, and abandonment in our lives and family. We become accepted in the Beloved and favored above all others where we were previously rejected. **Psalm 45:7.**

23

PRAYERS

1. Every seed and root of rejection in my foundation driving away my divine helpers, be uprooted by fire, in the name of Jesus.

2. Every spirit of Beelzebub, Lord of the flies, in my foundation that is magnetizing rejection to my life, die by fire.

3. Every evil smell and mouth odor from my foundation, repelling my helpers, be purged by the fire of God and flushed out by the blood of Jesus.

4. Holy Ghost fire, purge every rottenness and filthiness in my foundation attracting flies.

By Giving Us Double For Our Shame

God does a new thing by giving us double blessings for our shame:

"For your shame ye shall have double; and for confusion they shall rejoice in their portion: therefore in their land they shall possess the double: everlasting joy shall be unto them." Isaiah 61:7.

Our Lord Jesus was put to shame and disgraced so that we do not have to live with or tolerate shame and disgrace in any way, shape, or form. Jesus, our Kinsman-Redeemer, covers our nakedness with His Robe of Righteousness, taking away our shame just like Boaz, Ruth's kinsman-redeemer did for her.

"And he said, Who art thou? And she answered, I am Ruth thine handmaid: spread therefore thy skirt over thine handmaid; for thou art a near kinsman." Ruth 3:9.

PRAYERS

1. Shame, your time is up so you must expire in my life today.

2. Blood of Jesus go deep into my foundation and uproot every seed, tree, and root of nakedness.

3. Every arrow of shame, reproach and disgrace, backfire.

4. Every power sowing garments of shame, reproach, and disgrace into my life, fall down and die.

5. Every owner of evil load of shame and disgrace appear, carry your load and go.

6. Glory of God cover my nakedness, in the name of Jesus.

24

By Having Mercy on Us

"For a small moment have I forsaken thee; but with great mercies will I gather thee. In a little wrath I hid my face from thee for a moment; but with everlasting kindness will I have mercy on thee, saith the LORD thy Redeemer." Isaiah 54:7-8.

Jesus had mercy and compassion on the widow of Nain, whose only child had died, and raised him from the dead. **Luke 7:12-15.** He also had mercy on Bartimeus, the blind man who cried out desperately to Him for help and healed his blindness:

"Jesus thou Son of David have mercy on me." Mark 10:47.

Today as you too cry out to Him for mercy, He will hear your cry; have mercy on you; and answer you speedily in Jesus name. Then your life will become a living testimony in the name of Jesus.

PRAYERS
1. O Lord, let your mercy speak into every department of my life.
2. Mercy of God speak into my life. Speak into my ....
a) marriage   b) career   c) ministry   d) health
3. O Lord, arise in your power as God and change the rules for my sake.
4. O Lord, anchor your mercy to my head today, in the name of Jesus.
5. O Lord, where I am a lawful captive, arise in your mercy and set me free.
6. Where I have no voice, mercy of God, speak on my behalf. (Repeat over and over, "Mercy of God, speak for me.")

By Wiping Away Tears

God in His word has promised to wipe away all tears.

"And God shall wipe away all tears from their eyes; and there shall be no more death, neither shall there be any more pain: for the former things are passed away." Revelation 21:4.

He does a new thing in a person's life by wiping away tears. God wiped away the tears of King Hezekiah by healing him of sickness and adding fifteen more years to his life. **2 King 20:5.** He wiped away the tears of the Israelites when they cried to Him and delivered them from over 400 years of oppression in Egypt. **Exodus 3:9.**

Today the Holy Spirit is interceding for you and will bring to the Lord's remembrance your tears which are stored in His bottle. **Psalm 56:8.** Your tears are being wiped off even now, by the gentle hands of an ever loving Father. Your season of tears and sorrow is over and your season of joy and gladness is here. Receive it in Jesus name.

PRAYERS
1. My Father and my God, today arise in your mercy and compassion, and wipe away my tears, in the name of Jesus.
2. O Lord, let all my tears stored up in your bottle be turned to joy.
3. Every owner of evil load of tears and sorrow, carry your load.
4. I shall not cry, my enemy shall cry in my place instead.

By Recovering Lost Glory
Repeat out loud several times:
"I shall be a crown of glory, in the name of Jesus."

Your glory is the glory of God radiating in and through your life. It is the star quality that God has deposited in your life to make you shine and to enable you fulfill your divine purpose on earth. Glory is so important to a life that even God guards His own glory jealously and refuses to share it with anyone. **Isaiah 42:8.** Moses the servant of God, realizing this importance, refused to embark on the journey to the Promised Land unless God's glory and presence went with him. **Exodus 33:15.**

It is therefore a terrible thing when a person's glory is lost, exchanged, vandalized, captured, or tampered with in any way. The good thing is that no matter what has happened to your glory, you can still recover it. **Joel 2:25.** If you want to recover your lost glory today, then pray the following prayers with great aggression and desperation!

PRAYERS

1. Every man or woman, living or dead, using my glory to shine, release it and die, in the name of Jesus.

2. Every blanket covering my glory and the evil hands keeping it in place, catch fire and be roasted to ashes.

3. Power of God, restore the glory of my life back to me, in name.

4. O God, arise and fill my life with your glory.

5. Every internal captivity covering my glory come out and die.

6. Angels of the living God ransack the land of the living and the dead and recover my lost glory, in Jesus name.

7. Every witchcraft yoke against my glory, break and die.

8. Every power sitting on my glory, be unseated by fire.

9. My glory in captivity, jump out and locate me by fire.

10. My buried glory be exhumed now, be exhumed by fire.

By Making a Way Where There is No Way

Take this chorus with me please:

> God will make a way
> Where there seems to be no way
> He works in ways we cannot see
> He will make a way
> He will make a way

Jesus is the way, the truth, and the life. **John 14:6.** He creates a way where there is no way visible to man because He is the way. He brings the visible out of the invisible. Where human beings are saying that there is no way for you, today Lord Jesus will not only create a way but He will become the way for you to access what you want.

"And I will bring the blind by a way that they knew not; I will lead them in paths that they have not known: I will make darkness light before them, and crooked things straight. These things will I do unto them, and not forsake them." Isaiah 42:16.

"Thus saith the LORD, which maketh a way in the sea, and a path in the mighty waters." Isaiah 43:14.

PRAYERS
1. O Lord, make a way for me where there is no way.
2. O Lord, where men are saying there is a casting down, let there be a lifting up in my own life.
3. You my life refuse to be demoted in Jesus name.

By Opening Closed Doors

"And to the angel of the church in Philadelphia write; These things saith he that is holy, he that is true, he that hath the key of David, he that openeth, and no man shutteth; and shutteth, and no man openeth. I know thy works: behold I have set before thee an open door and no man can shut it." Revelation 3:7-8.

The Lord God is the one that opens and no one can shut. Just like there are doors in the physical realm, we also have doors in the spirit realm. These include doors of opportunities, advancement, and new things. To pass from one level to another in the spiritual realm you have to pass through doors or gates to get to the new level. The enemy often closes these doors against people especially at the edge of major breakthroughs. He can use anyone to close good doors against you, including your parents; wicked bosses and coworkers; wicked spouses or ex-spouses; and envious friends. For some the person that closed the door against them has even died.

I do not know what doors have been closed against you and by whom. What I do know is that regardless of who closed them or how long they have been closed today God is here to fling those doors open so that you can walk into the new arena that He has prepared for you. God is also the Creator so where no door exists, He can create new ones so that His people can go in and take hold of all that He has for them.

God not only opens closed doors but also removes the blockages, hindrances and embargos that normally surface when a new door of opportunity opens. Apostle Paul recognizing this said:

"For a great door and effectual is opened unto me, and there are many adversaries." 1 Corinthians 16:9.

28

Today as you pray the following prayers God will bulldoze every obstacle standing in your way and push you into the new things that He has for you in the mighty name of Jesus.

PRAYERS

1. My Father and My Lord, arise and open unto me all good doors that the enemy has closed against my life.

2. Every blockage at the edge of my breakthrough, crumble.

3. Every evil gateman standing at the gate of my breakthrough, catch fire.

4. Every evil power closing my doors of breakthroughs on me, die.

5. Season of opportunities and fulfillment open for me in Jesus name.

6. Doors of favor open for me now, in Jesus name.

7. Every embargo placed on my progress, break by fire.

By Divine Intervention

God can intervene directly by supernaturally stretching forth His hand from heaven to help. This is what happened to me some years back. The Lord intervened by giving me a prayer. As I prayed it, He intervened speedily in my situation. The prayer is:

O Lord, stretch forth your hand from heaven and remove us from this country.

As you too pray this prayer, God will stretch forth His hand from heaven and intervene in your situation mightily in Jesus name.

Another time Lord Jesus came to visit me in my hospital room and that day my medical situation turned around for God. The doctors called me a miracle. Jesus indeed delights in doing miracles in our lives.

God is sovereign and supreme and can intervene in any way that He sees fit. He can intervene directly like He did in my case. He can use angels like He did for Lot. **Genesis 19:15-17.** He did the same for Peter in the book of Acts. **Acts 12:1-11.** In the case of Paul and Silas, He released the earthquake of deliverance to set them free. **Acts 16:25.**

PRAYERS

1. Divine breakthroughs and joy locate me by fire in Jesus name.
2. O Lord, open the way to my breakthroughs and success (in my marriage, career, health, ministry, business) in Jesus name.
3. Earthquake of deliverance, bulldoze every hindrance to the manifestation of my new thing.
4. O God, arise and intervene in my situation today in Jesus name.
5. Holy Spirit anoint my prayers to move the hand of God of the suddenlies, in Jesus name.
6. Holy Ghost fire burn every garment of reproach fashioned for me to ashes.
7. Every power assigned to kill my laughter, you are a liar, die.
8. I apply the blood of Jesus to break all curses working against my finances, in Jesus name.
9. Curses and covenants of satanic delay break, in the name of Jesus.
10. I position myself by fire for divine intervention.
11. O Lord, arise in your power and intervene on my behalf today.
12. Thank you Lord for intervening in my situation.

By Divine substitution

In **Isaiah 43:3-4,** the Bible clearly says that the Lord does a new thing by giving lives in exchange for our lives.

"For I am the LORD thy God, the Holy One of Israel, thy Saviour: I gave Egypt for thy ransom, Ethiopia and Seba for thee. Since thou wast precious in my sight, thou hast been honourable, and I have loved thee: therefore will I give men for thee, and people for thy life."

Divine substitution can swing two ways. God can decide to use another person to replace His children when bad things happen. A classic example is Haman who was hung in the gallows that he had prepared for Mordecai. **Esther 7:10.** I pray that all your Hamans will die in your place this season.

God also substitutes His children for others when good things are being shared and there is not enough for everyone. He makes others to be disqualified so that His children can take their place and get the good thing. Today God will single you out for favor and greatness in the name of Jesus.

By Making Impossibilities Possible

"For thus saith the Lord, Ye shall not see wind, neither shall ye see rain; yet that valley shall be filled with water, that ye may drink, both ye, and your cattle, and your beasts." 2 Kings 3:17.

God does new things by doing things that are dumbfounding to the human mind and thinking. These things are seemingly impossible to men. He makes the supernatural to become the norm for His people. How else do you explain the testimony of a child that was born without eyes but the Lord gave her a beautiful pair of brown eyes? How do you explain the testimony of divine health of a young girl that the doctor's diagnosed with the worse type of sickle cell anemia at birth? She is now a young woman and has never been sick simply because God spoke and said "This sickness is not unto death but for the glory of God?" John 11:4. Surely, with these kinds of testimonies, you too will agree with me that truly:

"With God nothing shall be impossible." Luke 1:37.

By Fighting Your Battles For You

"The Lord shall fight for you, and ye shall hold your peace." Exodus 14:14.

"So shall they fear the name of the LORD from the west, and his glory from the rising of the sun. When the enemy shall come in like a flood, the Spirit of the LORD shall lift up a standard against him." Isaiah 59:19

He reveals the secrets of the enemy. 2 King 6:8-12. He can even turn your enemies against each other so that they destroy themselves for your sake. 2 Chronicles 20: 22-24. Also, He can command the elements to fight rather than cooperate with your enemies as He did for Joshua. Joshua 10:13-14. He will do this for you this season.

When God fights for you and destroys your enemies, then you will have all round peace which will give you the impetus for accelerated progress and prosperity like He did this Solomon after He destroyed the enemies of his father David. 1 Chronicles 22:9; 2 Chronicles 9:22-28.

I do not know what battles are confronting you but today I hear the Lord saying to you very clearly:

"Be still and know that I am God." Psalm 46:10.

By Stopping the Enemy before He Stops You

Please take this chorus with me:

Let God arise and his enemies be scattered
Let God arise and His enemies be scattered
Let God arise and his enemies be scattered
Let God, Let God arise

God does a new thing by stopping the devil and his demons from being able to carry out their harassment in our lives as before.   At the name of Jesus they are forced to bow. **Isaiah 43:20.**

"Behold, they shall surely gather together, but not by me: whosoever shall gather together against thee shall fall for thy sake." Isaiah 54:15.

This was the case with Daniel. He was delivered from the mouth of the lion and the lion ended up eating up all his enemies. **Daniel 6:24.**

One of the ways that God stops our enemies before they stop us is by equipping us to fight effectively and to win.

"Blessed be the LORD my strength which teacheth my hands to war, and my fingers to fight." Psalm 144:1-3.

By Helping You

The Lord does a new thing in our lives by helping us in our time of need. **Hebrews 4:16.**

"The Lord is my helper. And I will not fear what man shall do unto me." Hebrews 13:6.

He has promised to help us. All that we need to do is ask His help.

"Fear thou not; for I am with thee: be not dismayed; for I am thy God: I will strengthen thee; yea, I will help thee; yea, I will uphold thee with the right hand of my righteousness." Isaiah 41:10.

By Breaking Yokes

"And it shall come to pass in that day, that his burden shall be taken away from off thy shoulder, and his yoke from off thy neck, and the yoke shall be destroyed because of the anointing." Isaiah 10:27.

It is God's power that destroys the enemy's yokes in our lives. **Jeremiah 30:8.** Jesus Christ, the "Anointed One" is the yoke breaker and burden lifter.

An evil yoke is an evil load hanging on your destiny. It is a satanic rope tying you to problems. It is an evil ladder energizing and keeping your problems in place. It is the oppression of the enemy upon your life. It is the power suppressing elevation, progress, and growth in a person's life. Evil yokes are the witchcraft chains, ropes, and padlocks that bind a person's life pegging it to one spot for years.

Evil yokes keep bondages in place in a person's life. They make good things to slip away from a person's hands. A yoke may be targeted at specific areas of a person's life such as health, marriage, finances, business, career, or education.

When evil yokes are broken, affliction is taken away, and there is deliverance from oppression. An avalanche of new things usually follows such deliverance.

PRAYERS

1. Every witchcraft yoke assigned against my glory, break and die.
2. Every power yoking my life to problems (name the problem one by one) break and die.
3. Every evil rope tying my life down, break and release me now.
4. Evil hands working against my progress, wither by fire.
5. Every yoke of............ (Pick from the under listed) break by fire.
(a) Rising and falling   (b) Poverty   (c) Stagnancy   (d) Demotion
(e) Backwardness   (f) Failure   (g) Affliction   (h) Infirmity
(i) Satanic delay   (j) Slow progress (k) Untimely death
6. Anything representing me in the demonic realm, I withdraw your representation.
17. I withdraw any mandate given to any power, personality or spirit to afflict my life.

CHAPTER 5

FOR WHOM DOES GOD DO NEW THINGS?

"The Spirit of the Lord GOD is upon me; because the LORD hath anointed me to preach good tidings unto the meek; he hath sent me to bind up the brokenhearted, to proclaim liberty to the captives, and the opening of the prison to them that are bound; To proclaim the acceptable year of the LORD, and the day of vengeance of our God; to comfort all that mourn; To appoint unto them that mourn in Zion, to give unto them beauty for ashes, the oil of joy for mourning, the garment of praise for the spirit of heaviness; that they might be called trees of righteousness, the planting of the LORD, that he might be glorified." Isaiah 61:1-3.

God is sovereign so He has the final say in every situation. Therefore He can do new things for anyone however and whenever He chooses. Nevertheless, there are certain qualities, that when present, can provoke God to do new things in a person's life. We will now look at these qualities.

His Chosen Ones
God does new things for His chosen ones.

"The beast of the field shall honor me, the dragons and the owls: because I give waters in the wilderness, and rivers in the desert, to give drink to my people, my chosen." Isaiah 43:20.

These include His children and His servants. They are God's own who carry His blood, His DNA:

"But now thus saith the LORD that created thee, O Jacob, and he that formed thee, O Israel, Fear not: for I have redeemed thee, I have called thee by thy name; thou art mine" Isaiah 43:1.

"And when ye see this, your heart shall rejoice, and your bones shall flourish like an herb: and the hand of the LORD shall be known

34

toward his servants, and his indignation toward his enemies." Isaiah 66:14.

God delights in doing new things for those that know Him, that are His children, and not those of the devil. You get to know Him by getting born again. **(Please see the steps for getting born again at the end of this book).** This makes you a member of Jesus' family. Jesus said His family consists of those who know the will of God and do it. **Luke 8:19-21.**

The Humble and Contrite Hearted

God exalts the humble and brings down the proud. **Luke 18:14.** He hates the proud but shows mercy to the contrite in heart. God's mercy provokes new things.

"For thus saith the high and lofty One that inhabiteth eternity, whose name is Holy; I dwell in the high and holy place, with him also that is of a contrite and humble spirit, to revive the spirit of the humble, and to revive the heart of the contrite ones. For I will not contend for ever, neither will I be always wroth: for the spirit should fail before me, and the souls which I have made." Isaiah 57:14-15.

The Righteous and the Holy

"For the eyes of the Lord run to and fro throughout the whole earth to shew himself strong in the behalf of them whose heart is perfect towards him." 2 Chronicles 16:9.

"In righteousness shalt thou be *established*: thou shalt be far from oppression; for thou shalt not fear: and from terror; for it shall not come near thee." Isaiah 54:14.

The righteous are those that live right before God. They are the godly ones that honor God by their actions and lifestyle. They worship God in truth and holiness. The Bible mentions some people who walked righteous and blameless before God. God in return did new and unique things in their lives. A good example is Job who lost everything including all his children but God restored all that he lost back to him in multiples. **Job 1:1-5; Job 2:3; Job 42:12-16.** Others include the parents of John the Baptist, Zacharias and Elisabeth, whom the Bible described in the following passage:

35

"And they were both righteous before God, walking in all the commandments and ordinances of the Lord blameless." Luke 1:6.

After many years of barrenness, God did a new thing by giving them a son in their old age, John the Baptist, who had the privilege of being the one that was sent to prepare the way for Christ's coming. **Luke 1:17.**

The Bible clearly teaches us that without holiness no man shall see God. **Hebrews 12:14.** New things spring forth in God's presence. Since you cannot enter God's presence without holiness, it follows that without holiness, new things will be far away.

"And an highway shall be there, and a way, and it shall be called The way of holiness; the unclean shall not pass over it; but it shall be for those: the wayfaring men, though fools, shall not err therein." Isaiah 35:8.

The God Fearing

"What man is he that feareth the Lord? Him shall he teach in the way that he shall choose. His soul shall dwell at ease: and his seed shall inherit the earth." Psalm 25:12.

From the scripture above we are told that the God fearing shall inherit new things on earth. God visited Cornelius and did new things in his life, even though he was not a Jew, because he was godly and feared God. As a result of this, he and his household became the first gentiles to receive salvation. **Acts 10:1-48.**

Those that fear God are privy to His secrets. These secrets are beneficial revelations, which usher in new things into such lives. Revelation brings divine direction, repositioning, and relocation which puts you at the right place at the right time. The result could be phenomenon blessings and success. This is because it shows you where to cast your net in the ocean of life for new things to spring forth in your life.

We see this is the life of Peter the Apostle, and his team of fishermen. They toiled all night and caught no fish. At Jesus' command they cast their net a second time and caught so much fish that it took two boats to carry it. This was indeed a new thing that God was doing in their lives because by the end of the day they had a new calling of being fishers of men. **Luke 5:4-11.**

36

As you too pray the prayer below, God will reposition your life for success in Jesus name:

O Lord, I do not want to fish on my own. Please, show me where to cast my net in the ocean of life so that I can catch *good* fish.

Those That Wait Upon the Lord

God does new things for those who continuously seek Him. These are those who regardless of what is going on around them refuse to be discouraged or to resort to human wisdom and manipulations. They choose instead, through fasting and prayers, to wait upon the Lord. God promises them victory and that they will not be put to shame. **Isaiah 49:23.**

"But they that wait upon the Lord shall renew their strength; they shall mount up with wings as eagles; they shall run, and not be weary; and they shall walk, and not faint." Isaiah 40:31.

The Afflicted and Oppressed

"O thou afflicted, tossed with tempest, and not comforted, behold, I will lay thy stones with fair colours, and lay thy foundations with sapphires. And I will make thy windows of agates, and thy gates of carbuncles, and all thy borders of pleasant stones. And all thy children shall be taught of the LORD; and great shall be the peace of thy children. In righteousness shalt thou be established: thou shalt be far from oppression; for thou shalt not fear: and from terror; for it shall not come near thee." Isaiah 54:11-14.

God may have allowed affliction in your life for a season to refine you and prepare you for new things. **Isaiah 48:10.** Today, He is doing a new thing by saying to those that have been weeping "Weep no more." To those that have been disgraced, He is saying "My grace is available today and it is sufficient for you." **2 Corinthians 12:9.**

The Rejected and the Desolate

For those that have been rejected and condemned to a life of desolation, God is doing a new thing. Today, He is saying to you, "You are accepted in the Beloved." **Ephesians 1:6.** This means that you are accepted in Our Lord Jesus Christ who was rejected for our sake. God is saying that He is changing your name and your story today so that where you were rejected before you shall not only be accepted, but celebrated:

"Thou shalt no more be termed Forsaken; neither shall thy land any more be termed desolate, but thou shalt be called Hephzibah, and thy land Beulah: for the LORD delighteth in thee, and thy land shall be married." Isaiah 62:3-5.

The Captives

"To open the blind eyes, to bring out the prisoners from the prison, and them that sit in darkness out of the prison house." Isaiah 42:7.

For anyone that is in bondage, it is a new day and a new dawn because God is doing a new thing. Our Lord Jesus has come to set the captives free. **Luke 4:18.** He has also taken all captivity captive. **Ephesians 4:8.** Even if it is your own actions that have put you in captivity, today He will set you free because He has come to set even the lawful captives, the captive of the terrible, and the captive of the mighty free. **Isaiah 49:24-26.**

PRAYER: Where I am a lawful captive, O Lord by your mercy, arise and set me free.

His Witnesses

"Ye are my witnesses, saith the LORD, and my servant whom I have chosen: that ye may know and believe me, and understand that I am he: before me there was no God formed, neither shall there be after me." Isaiah 43:10.

God's witnesses are those whose lives testify of His goodness to others. They are living testimonies. Not only that, they are ever willing to open their months and testify of God's goodness in their lives to others. Testifying of

38

God's goodness to others flings the door open for God to do even more glorious things in their lives thereby keeping their testimonies ever fresh.

"The Testimony of Jesus is the spirit of prophesy." Revelation 19:10.

You should not wait until God does big things in your life before you testify. Rather as you obediently and faithfully testify of the little things that God is doing in your life this season, He will do even much greater miracles in your life in Jesus name. **Job 8:7.** He will indeed turn your whole life into a living testimony.

Those That Have Eyes to See What God is Doing

"Seeing many things, but thou observest not; opening the ears, but he heareth not." Isaiah 42:20.

You have to train your spiritual eyes to see what God is doing because it is easier to take hold of the new things that God is doing if you can see them in the spirit realm. Then all you have to do is pray them into physical manifestation. This entails having your inner spiritual eyes awakened so that they can see things while they are still brewing in the spiritual realm before they even manifest in the physical realm. This was the lifestyle of our Lord Jesus who said that He did only what He saw His Father doing and worked when His Father worked. **John 5:17, 19.**

The Prophet Elisha operated in this realm also. He prayed for God to open the eyes of his servant so that he too could see into the spiritual realm and God did. **2 Kings 6:17.** Today, we too can ask God to open our eyes. It is not business as usual. God is moving and doing new things. We should move with the cloud of glory. We need our spiritual eyes open to keep up with Him and partake in these new things which are meant for our benefit.

Those Who Have the Ears of the Learned

God is a spirit so for you to hear Him, your spirit man has to be awakened and your spiritual ears tuned to His frequency. As His sheep, you are supposed to hear what He is saying but spiritual deafness can prevent you from hearing and recognizing His voice.

"My sheep hear my voice, and I know them, and they follow me." John 10:27.

We see our Lord Jesus say over and over in the Bible:

"He that hath ears to hear, let him hear." Matthew 11:15: Revelation 3:6.

From this we understand that the ability to hear what is going on in the spirit realm is pivotal to keying into the new things that God wants to do in our lives. Just like you hear through your physical ear, you also have spiritual ears that enable you to hear in the spirit realm. Inability to hear God poses a big problem as it is much easier to receive new things from Him when you can hear, understand, and follow His instructions.

Those that Overcome

The power to overcome has been given to every child of God. God does new things and gives new things to His children that overcome through faith, wisdom, and patience. These new things include new crowns, white robes, new names, new opportunities, and new provision. They are also given power over the nations; the ability to be pillars in God's house; and the ability to sit with Jesus on His throne. **Revelation 3:12, 21.** In fact, God promises that they shall inherit all things.

"He that overcometh shall inherit all things; and I will be his God, and he shall be my son." Revelation 21:7.

CHAPTER 6

WHY IS GOD DOING A NEW THING?

To Keep Covenants Made With His People

God is doing a new thing because He is the covenant keeping God who honors His agreements and contracts with man. **Psalm 89:34.** He even honors His word that has gone forth out of His mouth above His name. **Psalm 138:2.** His covenant with His children is forever.

"For the mountains shall depart, and the hills be removed; but my kindness shall not depart from thee, neither shall the covenant of my peace be removed, saith the LORD that hath mercy on thee." Isaiah 54:10

It is because God is still honoring His covenants with Abraham that even today, we are able to tap into the blessings that flow from those covenants through Christ. What an awesome God we serve!

"Christ hath redeemed us from the curse of the law, being made a curse for us: for it is written, Cursed is every one that hangeth on a tree: That the blessing of Abraham might come on the Gentiles through Jesus Christ; that we might receive the promise of the Spirit through faith." Galatians 3:13-14.

To Declare His glory

The Bible says we are created for this purpose. God does new things to declare His glory in and through our lives. We are created for His pleasure and to show forth His glory and praise on earth.

"Even every one that is *called by my name*: **for I have created him for my glory, I have formed him; yea, I have made him." Isaiah 43:1.**

"When Jesus heard that, he said, This sickness is not unto death, but for the glory of God, that the Son of God might be glorified thereby." John 11:4.

41

Our lives should be witnesses of the great and glorious things that God is doing on earth today.

To Show His Faithfulness

"Know therefore that the Lord thy God, he is God, the faithful God, which keepeth covenant and mercy with them that love him and keep his commandments to a thousand generation." Deuteronomy 7:9.

"Let us hold fast the profession of our faith, without wavering; (for he is faithful that promised)." Hebrew 10:23.

God is faithful. He keeps His promises. He never lies or forgets. This is why the Bible says that with God, there is:

"No variableness neither shadow of turning." James 1:17.

Once He promises you something He delivers. **Number s 23:19.** He not only watches over His word to perform it but actually hastens to perform it. **2 Thessalonians 3:3.**

To Display His Awesome Power

God does new things as a way of displaying His awesome power as the living God. He did something that had never been done before in setting His children, the Israelites, free from four hundred years of captivity in Egypt. He hardened the heart of Pharaoh so that he refused to let them go. God then swung into action. He parted the Red Sea and led His children safely through it. Then He turned around and buried Pharaoh and his army in the Red Sea when they attempted to cross over in hot pursuit of the Israelites. God indeed gave His people the victory and got the glory. Alleluia!!! **Exodus 9:16.**

Today, the Lord will do the same for you. He will bring His awesome power to bear on stubborn pursuing powers refusing to let you go and fulfill your God given purpose. I declare over your life, you shall fulfill your divine purpose in the name of Jesus.

CHAPTER 7

HINDRANCES TO THE MANIFESTATION OF NEW THINGS

There are certain factors that can prevent or hinder the new things that God wants to do in our lives from manifesting. God likes to do new things in the lives of His children but there are certain things that He hates. These are clearly stated in His word, the Bible. Doing these things ties up His hands from releasing new things into our lives.

Also, there are certain things that God wants us to let go of. Holding on to these old things can prevent the manifestation of the new things that God want to do for us.

"Remember ye not the former things, neither consider the things of old." Isaiah 43:18.

Old things have passed away. Behold all things have become new." 2 Corinthians 5:17.

Apostle Paul talking of this said:

"Brethren, I count not myself to have apprehended: but this one thing I do, forgetting those things which are behind, and reaching forth unto those things which are before, I press toward the mark for the prize of the high calling of God in Christ Jesus." Philippians 3:13-14.

There are also some doors that are currently open in various areas of our lives that need to be closed before new doors can open.

We must let go of the past and take hold of the new things that the Lord is doing now. These are the new things that He has pronounced in the spirit and declared to us.

"Behold, the former things are come to pass, and new things do I declare: before they spring forth I tell you of them." Isaiah 42:9.

43

Not doing this will allow the past to choke our now and our future. That will not be your portion in Jesus name. It is just like in the Parable of the Sower when the cares of this world choked the word of God, the new seed that the sower planted. **Luke 8:14.**

Now let us look at some of the things that we should let go off if we want new things to spring forth in our lives.

Unconfessed sins

The Bible tells us that if we hide our sins instead of confessing them we will not prosper.

"He that covereth his sins shall not prosper: but whoso confesseth and forsaketh them shall have mercy." Proverbs 28:13.

It further says that God is able to help us in whatsoever situation that we find ourselves but that sin can prevent Him from helping us. **Isaiah 59:1.**

However, no matter how hideous the sin is, once we have confessed and repented of it, and done any required restitution, we should let go and leave it behind us. This is because as soon as we confess and forsake our sins, they are cast into the sea of forgetfulness by our ever merciful Savior. **Micah 7:19.** We should learn to forgive ourselves once God has forgiven us, walk in that freedom, and move on.

Old Mind Sets

The Bible says that God's ways are not our ways but much higher than our ways and His thoughts much higher than our thoughts. **Isaiah 55:8-9.** Old mind sets and thought patterns have to go or they will hinder the new things that God is doing. The old carnal way of thinking is contrary to God's thinking pattern. **Romans 8:7.** The Bible commands us to pull down all such thoughts and force them to conform to God's thinking pattern. We do this by pulling down every high thing that wants to exalt itself against the knowledge of God in any area of our lives:

"Casting down imaginations, and every high thing that exalteth itself against the knowledge of God, and bringing into captivity every thought to the obedience of Christ." 2 Corinthians 10:5.

44

We also have to put on the mind of Christ. **Philippians 2:5**. We do this by allowing the word of God to constantly renew our mind. **Romans 12:2**. This is necessary because satan is constantly battling our minds.

Lack of Forgiveness

Inability to forgive others hinders prayers and without answered prayers there can be no new things. God expects us to forgive others even as He forgives us.

"And when ye stand praying, forgive, if ye have ought against any: that your Father also which is in heaven may forgive you your trespasses. But if you do not neither will your Father which is in heaven forgive your trespasses." Mark 11:25-26.

Unregenerated Hearts

These are hearts that are full of negative feelings such as anger, bitterness, envy and jealousy, and lack of forgiveness. These will hinder the new things that God has ordained for you. A heart like that ties up your hands and prevents you from taking hold of your new things. You will be looking at the table prepared for you by the Lord before your enemies but you will not be able to eat from it. It will also give you "slippery blessing" that keep slipping out of your hands.

King David's brothers learnt this lesson the hard way when God rejected them and chose David to be king because of the purity of his heart. **1 Samuel 16:7-13.**

Carnality

"For ye are yet carnal: for whereas there is among you envying, and strife, and divisions, are ye not carnal, and walk as men?" 1 Corinthians 3:3.

The Bible teaches us that the carnal mind is enmity with God. **Romans 8:7**. God is a spirit and we must relate to Him as spirit beings. Our flesh hinders us from doing this and so keeps us from receiving new things from Him.

One major source of carnality is our old unfruitful lifestyle. **Colossian 3: 5-10**. A good example of carnality is anger. It prevented Moses from entering the Promised Land and partaking of its goodness. **Numbers 20:7-12.** It will stop you too if you do not deal with it in your life now.

Are you still engaging in fornication, adultery, talkativeness, perversion, drunkenness, and the like? These are the works of the flesh mentioned in **Galatians 5:19-21**. They abort new things in a person's life.

Which places do you go? Whose company do you keep? What discussions do you engage in? Will they build up your faith to enable you to receive the new things that God is doing or will they kill your faith and abort the new things that God has in the offering for you?

Forsaking Basic Christian Disciplines

To mature and be able to take possession of the new things that God has for you, you need to be spiritually disciplined. There is no getting around this. You have to do your quiet time, prayers, warfare, vigils, fasting, church attendance, tithing and other Christian disciplines regularly. For example, God is not going to give a wife to "a boy" who will ill-treat her because he has no spiritual discipline. Not when there is no scripture reading, no night vigils, no fasting, and no prayers. No integrity or character.

Spiritually, you need to grow and become mature. **Hebrews 5:11-14; 1 Timothy 4:8.** You have to become a firebrand Christian so that spiritual armed robbers and other day and night marauders do not come in unchecked and steal the new things that God is doing in your life.

Mistakes and Errors from the Past

Paul the Apostle in the Bible was a murderer who was an accessory to the death of Stephen, a deacon in the early church. **Acts7:58-60.** Moses, the servant of God was also a murderer. **Exodus 2:12.** King David murdered Uriah because he lusted for his wife, Bathsheba. **2 Samuel 11:4-15.** These giants in the Lord, though murderers, did not allow the heinous shadows from their past to stop them from pressing into the new things that God had ordained for their lives. You should emulate them and not allow your past to waste your now and your tomorrow. Today, you too should pick up the pieces of your life and go ahead to become all that God has ordained for you to be in Jesus name. Greatness is available and is yours. Receive it in Jesus name.

Anxiety

The Bible teaches us that worry and anxiety are unprofitable exercises because they cannot make our situation better but actually worsens it. **Luke 12:22-31.** It commands us instead to be anxious for nothing but to seek solution to our problems through prayers and thanksgiving:

"Be careful for nothing; but in everything by prayer, and supplication with thanksgiving let your requests be made know unto God." Philippians 4:6.

Doubt and Unbelief

If you want to see new things manifest in your life you should believe what God has told you rather than doubting.

"And blessed is she that believed: for there shall be a performance of those things which were told her from the Lord." Luke 1:45.

Abraham did and his new thing manifested as after 25 years of waiting. Isaac, the child that God promised him, came. **Romans 4:20.** The Bible records that unbelief made Jesus unable to do great works in His hometown of Capernaum. **Matthew 13:58.** Familiarity they say breeds contempt. The people saw Him as a mere man, who grew up in their midst and not as God that can do all things. **Matthew 13:54-57.** What about you? Are you getting overfamiliar with God?

The Bible also clearly teaches that a doubtful person is unstable and will not receive new things from the Lord. **James 1:6-7.** Therefore, to receive new things from God you have to deal with doubt and unbelief because if you do not, they will abort the new things that God has for you.

"For verily I say unto you, that whosoever shall say unto this mountain, Be thou removed and be thou cast into the sea; and shall not doubt in his heart, but shall believe that those things which he saith shall come to pass; he shall have whatsoever he saith." Mark 11:23.

Faulty Foundation

"If the foundations be destroyed, what can the righteous do?" Psalm 11:3.

A bad foundation cannot sustain good things. A major cause of bad foundation is idolatry, which is the worship of anyone or anything besides God the Father, God the Son, and God the Holy Spirit, through Jesus Christ. An idol is anything that you put first before God. It opens the door for the enemy to come into a person's life to kill, steal, and destroy. **John 10:10.**

The opened door should be closed and the faulty foundation repaired through deliverance, targeted prayers, and fasting so that it is strengthened and becomes strong enough to attract and sustain new things.

Prayerlessness

"Therefore I say unto you, what things soever ye desire, when ye pray, believe that ye receive them and ye shall have them." Mark 11:24.

We are encouraged to pray always and to pray without season. **Luke 18:1, 21:36. 1 Thessalonian 5:17.** We are also to pray in our own understanding and in the spirit. **1 Corinthians 14:15.** God expects us to call unto Him if we want Him to single us out for breakthroughs and an avalanche of new things.

"Call unto me, and I will answer thee, and show thee great and mighty things, which thou knowest not." Jeremiah 33:3.

We should be like the widow that pestered the unjust judge until she got what she wanted. **Luke 18:1-8.**

In **Isaiah 62:1-7,** the intercessors were told to pray until a new thing happened in Jerusalem. We should emulate them. We should pray until there is a positive change in our situation and new things begin to manifest. These new things will not manifest if we relent before they are fully in place.

Impatience

Impatience will make us lose out on the new things that God has in store for us. We should be patient like Father Abraham who waited for 25 years for his son, Isaac, to manifest without wavering in faith.

"That ye be not slothful but followers of them who through faith and patience inherit the promises. That ye be not slothful, but followers of them who through faith and patience inherit the promises. …….. And so, after he had patiently endured, he obtained the promise." Hebrew 6:12, 15.

Ungodly & Unholy Lifestyle

"For bodily exercise profiteth little: but godliness is profitable unto all things, having promise of the life that now is, and of that which is to come." 1 Timothy 4:8.

"Follow peace with all men, and holiness, without which no man shall see the Lord." Hebrews 12:14.

From the scripture verses above, we see that without holiness no man can see God. New things spring forth in the presence of God. Therefore, we have to be holy because God is holy and it takes holiness to access His presence to obtain the new things that we desire in life.

Quitting

Lack of perseverance and giving in to discouragement, frustration, and anxiety can make you to quit like the prophet Elijah did. God still had a lot of new things that He wanted Elijah to do for Him. We know this because God had him commission Elisha, Jehu, and Hazael to do these things instead before he ascended to heaven. **1 King 19:14-18.**

Just like in the case of Elijah, many new things that God started in the lives of many of His children have been aborted on the altar of discouragement, fear, frustration, and impatience. The devil specializes in fighting believers and stealing from them with these weapons. You must refuse to surrender to the enemy because this grieves the heart of God:

"And Jesus said unto him, No man having put his hand to the plough and looking back is fit for the kingdom of God." Luke 9:62.

"Now the just shall live by faith: but if any man draws back, my soul shall have no pleasure in him." Hebrews 10:38.

49

Negative Confessions

Our confessions, both positive and negative, carry great power. The Bible says that life and death are in the power of the tongue. **Proverbs 18:21.** It goes further to say that the words that we speak can condemn or justify us before God and men. **Matthew 12:37.**

God Himself says that the words that He speaks never return to him void but accomplishes whatever purpose that He intends them to. **Isaiah 55:11.** We are also told that God spoke all things into being by the power of his words. **Hebrew 1:3.** God has said that whatever we speak to His hearing, He will bring to pass in our lives. **Numbers 14:28.** The Israelites that left Egypt perished in the wilderness without making it to the Promised Land, because they kept murmuring and confessing that they would die in the wilderness. **Numbers 14:27-30.**

Our spoken words determine what God does or does not do in our lives. Therefore, we should not make negative confessions as they will abort the new things that God wants to do. Rather daily, we should confess positive words from the Bible that pertain to the challenges that we are going through over our lives. For example, instead of saying "I am too old to have a child" you could say, "I am planted in the house of the Lord. I shall flourish and I shall still bring forth fruit in old age." **Psalm 92:14.**

Fear

Fear is the opposite of faith. It means that because of our present circumstances, we are now doubting God's word to do new things in our lives. A double minded man cannot receive anything from God. **James 1:8.** No matter what you are going through, do not allow fear in your life. God is speaking to you today in the scripture below:

"Say to them that are of a fearful heart, Be strong, fear not: behold, your God will come with vengeance, even God with a recompense; he will come and save you." Isaiah 35:3-4.

You are calling God a liar when you allow fear to rule in your life. God hates that so much that He has prepared a place for the fearful in the Lake of fire. **Revelation 21:8.** Say:

"Fear, I bind you and I cast you out of my life. You will not land me in the Lake of fire in the name of Jesus."

Rebellion, and Disobedience

"To obey is better than sacrifice and to hearken than the fat of rams. For rebellion is as the sin of witchcraft, and stubbornness is as iniquity and idolatry." 1 Samuel 15:22-23.

Rebellion and disobedience will deny you of the new things that God wants to do in your life. God did a new thing in Israel by making Saul the first king of Israel. But he rebelled against God and His servant, Samuel. As a result of this, he and his posterity were removed forever from being king. **1 Samuel 15:23**. Make the following confessions:

1. **Rebellion will not deny me of my right to be king in the name of Jesus."**
2. Another will not take our position in Jesus name."

Ignorance

You may not be able to take hold of the new things that God has for you if you are ignorant. This includes ignorance of God and His ways; who you are in Christ Jesus; and who the devil is. Ignorance can result from laziness in studying the word of God and applying it to your life.

"Apply thine heart unto instruction, and thine ears to the words of knowledge." Proverbs 23:12.

It could also result from lack of understanding and discernment.

"My people perish are destroyed for lack of knowledge, because thou hast rejected knowledge, I will also reject thee." Hosea 4:6.

In the Bible, Peter the Apostle, out of ignorance tried to discourage our Lord Jesus from going to the cross where He was to die for the sins of man. This in effect would have aborted Jesus' purpose for coming to this world and the new thing that God wanted to do for mankind through His death on the Cross of Calvary. This was to bring redemption from sin, reconciliation of man to God, and salvation to all. Jesus viciously and vehemently fought back saying:

"But he (Jesus) turned and said unto Peter, Get thee behind me satan: thou art an offence unto me: for thou savorest not the things that be of God, but those that be of men." Matthew 16:23.

Lack of Wisdom

"Wisdom is the principal thing. In all thy getting get understanding."

If you want new things to continuous spring up in your life, then you should get wisdom. This kind of wisdom can only be found in Christ and His word.

"Through wisdom is an house builded; and by understanding it is established." Proverbs 24:3.

The good thing is that if you lack wisdom, you can always ask God for it. James 1:5.

Talkativeness

Talking indiscriminately can bring problems. James 1:26. When you have no control over your tongue you can end up giving secrets to your enemies which they can use against you. James 3:13. This can bring unnecessary warfare that aborts the new thing that God is doing. If not for the grace of God, Joseph would have fallen into this trap because he shared divine secrets about his life with household enemies and they almost truncated his glorious destiny. Genesis 37:4-11. Who are you sharing your divine beneficial secrets with today?

Having Idols in the Heart

Sometimes we hold on to things because they have become idols in our heart. We allow them to crowd out the still small voice of the Holy Spirit that is telling us the truth. Today that voice is saying "Release it. Let it go. I have a better plan and option. Trust me to know the best for you and to stand by you. Have I ever failed you? Have I ever misled you?"

This is particularly true in the area of relationships. As long as we are holding on to that unprofitable relationship, the new, beautiful, and fresh one that God has for us cannot manifest. We should therefore let go and let God. The hurt will heal. The disappointment and feeling of rejection will go away. It is better to deal with this temporary discomfort and reproach now than to have to endure a lifetime of shame, sorrow, tears, and regret. What is that idol that you are holding onto in your heart today? Release it to God, who is more than enough for you. He is your sufficiency.

Spirit of Slumber

"According as it is written, God hath given them the spirit of slumber, eyes that they should not see, and ears that they should not hear unto this day." Romans 11:7-9.

The spirit of slumber makes a person unable to see or to hear spiritually. This spiritual insensitive is dangerous because new things occur first in the spiritual realm before manifesting in the physical. So if you cannot see it while it is brewing in the spiritual realm, you may never possess it in the physical. Therefore, this spirit can deprive you of the new things that God wants to do in your life. **Isaiah 6:10.**

Instead of slumbering, we should have our spiritual ears opened as described below:

"He wakeneth morning by morning he wakeneth mine ear to hear as the learned." Isaiah 50:4

PRAYERS

1. Every evil thing programmed into my life to affect my life negatively now and in the future, I deprogram you by the power in the blood of Jesus.

2. Every evil hand from my past writing failure in my present and my future, be cut off and die.

3. Every agent of darkness using discouragement to steal the new things that God has for my life, die, in Jesus name.

4. I refuse to be cheated by the devil in the name of Jesus.

5. Everything in me working against the manifestation of my new things, come out and die, in the name of Jesus.

6. Spirit of slumber my life is not your candidate, die now.

7. O Lord, open my eyes that I may see, in the name of Jesus.

8. O Lord, open my ears that I may hear, in the name of Jesus.

9. Every power militating against God's best for my life, die by fire.

10. I damage my ignorance by the power in the blood of Jesus.

11. O Lord, thank you that according to Your word, we can ask for and receive wisdom if we lack it.

12. O Lord, pour your wisdom and your understanding upon me now.

13. Every evil arrow fired into my life, jump out and backfire.

14. Every owner of evil load, I summon you here, carry your load and go.

CHAPTER 8

ENEMIES OF THE NEW THINGS GOD IS DOING

Whenever God decides to do a new thing in a person's life, usually several enemies rise up to contend against it. Apostle Paul was a warrior in Gods' army who knew about such things and talking about this, he said:

"For a great door and effectual is opened unto me, and there are many adversaries." 1 Corinthians 16:9.

We will now take a look at the profile of some of these common enemies of the new things that God wants to do in our lives this season.

The Spirit of Herod

The spirit of Herod is the spirit that kills new things at infancy. **Matthew 2:1-18.** It seeks to terminate God's plans and purposes for a person's life. It directly opposes and attacks God's will and plans for such a life. This is the spirit that in a bid to kill Jesus, prompted King Herod to kill all the babies that were born in Israel at the time that Jesus was born. God delivered and preserved Jesus's life by sending Him away to Egypt. This spirit also kills people's God given dreams and visions.

The spirit of Herod works hand in hand with the spirit of divination, evil monitoring, and occultism. These evil spirits enable it to see and identify the special virtues and glory that these special children of God carry for the purpose of transforming and impacting their generation. At the command of their master, the devil, they make all attempts to kill these children so that they do not live to carry out their divine mandate. Death here can be spiritual or physical death.

The spirit of Herod often manifests in the activities of eaters of flesh and drinkers of blood. **Psalm 27:1-2.** We see this spirit in action when God raised Moses to deliver Israel from captivity after four hundred years of slavery in Egypt. The spirit of Herod rose up and made Pharaoh to kill all the children in Israel that were about Moses' age in a bid to kill Moses. God preserved His life. He took Moses out from amongst the people that He had called him to deliver and hid him in the palace of Pharaoh, a pagan king, who was a sworn enemy of his people to preserve his life. What a marvelous God we serve.

This spirit manifested also when Our Lord Jesus was born. He too was sought after by eaters of flesh and drinkers of blood led by King Herod. They did not want Him to fulfill His divine purpose which God clearly stated in His word both before and after His birth:

"For unto us this day in the City of David a Savior is born which is Christ the Lord." Luke 2:11.

PRAYER: Every spirit assigned to kill the new things that God is doing in my life, you have failed, die now, in the name of Jesus.

Spirit of Pisgah

This is the spirit of "almost there" or the "near success" syndrome. It allows you to come very close to getting the new thing that God has promised and then right before your eyes it evaporates and you are unable to possess it.

Moses experienced this in his divine assignment of leading the Israelites to the Promised Land. God took him to Mount Pisgah and showed him the Promised Land, but assured him that he would not enter it. **Deuteronomy 34:1-5.** True to God's word, Moses never made it there but died and was buried in the wilderness in the land of Moab. His servant Joshua ended up leading the people to the Promised Land. Close your eyes and pray these prayers:

1. Every power energizing the spirit of Pisgah in my life, die by fire, in the name of Jesus.
2. Every power assigned to prevent me from entering my Promised Land, die in the name of Jesus.
3. My Land of Promise will not be interrupted, in the name of Jesus.

The Spirit of Balaam

Balaam was a prophet that was hired to curse Israelites, God's children. **Numbers 22:1-6.** The spirit of Balaam represents satanic intermediaries that are hired to curse God's people. Curses limit goodness and can abort the new things that God wants to do in a person's life. Curses have to be broken

56

or they remain in effect from one generation to another. For example, if there is an ancestral curse of poverty operating in a family or community there can be no prosperity until such a curse is broken.

If your feet are cursed it will be very difficult for you to be established as they will ensure that you are never in the right place at the time. Instead, they will carry you to wrong places, wrong relationships, wrong jobs, and wrong locations. You will be getting to your place of blessing late. You will get there just as the new thing that is being distributed runs out.

If you are operating under a curse, you will be plagued by dreams of things finishing before your time or of missing your bus just by minutes. Also dreams of gates closing against you just as you are about to enter. Slippery blessing will be the order of the day because even when God releases good things to you, your hands cannot hold unto them and they slip off.

New things cannot manifest in such a life until such hands are passed through the fire of deliverance and washed and purged with the blood of Jesus.

PRAYERS

1. I command all curses issued against me to be smashed to pieces and broken.
2. I fire back every evil pronouncement uttered against me by poisonous tongues, in the name of Jesus.
3. O Lord, baptize my enemies with their evil plans against my life.
4. Every Balaam hired to curse me, fall after the order of Balaam in the name of Jesus.
5. Every evil tongue speaking against me, be cut off by the sword of Jehovah.
6. No weapon that is fashioned against me shall prosper, in Jesus name.
7. Every curse controlling and manipulating my life, break by the blood of Jesus.
8. Evil will not manifest in my life, in the name of Jesus.
9. Every curse pronounced upon my handiwork break by the blood of Jesus.
10. I challenge my hands with the fire of God.
11. I wash my hands with the blood of Jesus.
12. Every evil ladder keeping curses in place in my life catch fire.

The Spirit of Cain

"And a man's foes shall be they of his own household." Matthew 10:36.

This spirit of Cain is energized by household wickedness powers. It derives its name from Cain who killed his brother Abel out of Envy. **Genesis 4:6.** It is wickedness perpetuated by members of your immediate family against you. Perpetuators include close enemies such as cousins, parents, grand-parents, uncles, aunties, siblings, spouses, and in-laws. Even your own children could be the culprits.

The Bible is full of illustrations of this terrible and devastating spirit. Delilah, Samson's wife, sold him off to the Philistines, his arch enemies, who gouged out his eyes and brought about his untimely death. **Judges 16:16-21.** Rebekah, Esau's mother colluded with his brother Jacob to steal his birthright and the blessing meant for him as the first born. **Genesis 27.** Joseph's brothers that sold him into slavery in a foreign land out of envy. **Genesis 37:24-28.**

The testimony is told of a mother that brought her blind daughter for prayers. They were both given the following prayer to pray:

"Owner of evil load, carry your load."

As the prayers progressed, the daughter recovered her sight while the mother became blind. What really happened is that the mother was forced to carry her evil load as she was responsible for her daughter's blindness. Say:

The rod of the wicked shall not prosper in my life in the name of Jesus.

Another testimony is told of a wicked aunt who periodically stole her niece's under wears. She used these to bewitch and manipulate her niece. This manifested in terrible menstrual pains with fainting spells before marriage and in prolonged premature menopause and barrenness after marriage. Thank God for delivering her. Today, that same God will locate and deliver you from the spirit of Cain and its trademark household wickedness, in the name of Jesus. Receive your deliverance in Jesus name.

These things are real folks and they are devastating if not properly diagnosed and addressed through the ministry of deliverance. They can set you back years in the journey of life.

PRAYERS

1. By the power in the blood of Jesus, I separate myself from every landlord spirit, in the name of Jesus

2. I fire back every witchcraft arrow fired at me, in Jesus name.

3. Every power of my father's house that has sounded an alarm against my heart, fall down and die, in the name of Jesus.

4. Household wickedness powers destroying my life, die now.

5. Household wickedness powers fighting against me, buy your coffin.

6. Evil hands cutting off good things from my life, be cut off.

7. Every owner of evil load….. (Name them one by one including sickness, failure, insanity, rejection) carry your load in Jesus name.

8. Household wickedness powers of my father's house from my place of birth or origin trying to rewrite my destiny, fall down and die.

9. Every dragon running around in the garden of my life, fall down and die, in the name of Jesus.

10. I recover back everything that household wickedness powers have stolen from me and my family by the power in the blood of Jesus.

The Spirit of Goliath

The spirit of Goliath represents boasting, persistent, and unrepentant pursing powers. They are highly demonic strongmen that have great confidence in the demonic powers that they use to oppress others. These powers include voodoo, ancestral, witchcraft, familiar spirit, serpentine, marine, occult, and psychic powers.

"And the Philistine cursed David by his gods." 1 Samuel 17:43.

They make open threats against people just like the original Goliath did against God's children in the Bible. **1 Samuel 17:43-44.** They want to make you feel that their power is greater than the power of God that you carry.

PRAYERS

1. Power source of my enemies, dry up, in the name of Jesus.

2. Wicked powers from any source redesigning my life and destiny, die.

3. Goliath of my father's house fall down and die.

4. Goliath of my mother's house somersault and die, now.

59

Unfriendly Friends

This is another group of close enemies. They pretend to be your friends, eating and drinking with you, but behind you they destroy you and secretly engineer a lot of the problems that you encounter in life. Some are envious and wicked, while others attempt to cover up their inferiority complex with wickedness. Some of them deliberately give you bad advice just to abort the new things that God is doing in your life. The Bible warns us against such saying:

"Trust ye not in a friend, put ye not confidence in a guide: keep the doors of thy mouth from her that lieth in thy bosom." Micah 7:5.

PRAYERS:
1. Every unfriendly friend in my life, make mistakes that will advance my cause, in the name of Jesus.
2. O God, disappoint the expectation of the enemy over my life.
3. Fire of God, destroy and paralyze every agent and power of envy working to turn my glory to shame in the name of Jesus.
4. You unfriendly friends, depart from me, in the name of Jesus.
5. Every snare prepared for me by unfriendly friends catch your owner.
6. Let the power source of unfriendly friends be dissolved by fire.
7. Let all unfriendly friends be exposed and disgraced.
8. I recover back all that close enemies have stolen from me.

Anti-Glory Powers

"Arise, shine; for thy light is come, and the glory of the LORD is risen upon thee. For, behold, the darkness shall cover the earth, and gross darkness the people: but the LORD shall arise upon thee, and his glory shall be seen upon thee. And the Gentiles shall come to thy light, and kings to the brightness of thy rising." Isaiah 60:1-3.

These are powers that do not want the glory of God to manifest in and through your life. They do not want your glory to shine. Often they are evil authority figures around you that are manipulating your glory and your destiny.

It could be that wicked grandparent that has given you a bad hair style in the spirit realm. It could be that wicked pastor covering up your glory or that evil parent that has sold off all her children to witchcraft and occult powers and is using their glory to shine. It could be that demonic spouse or ex-spouse that keeps pressing your head down every time you try to lift it up. It could be that wicked boss or co-worker that wants to be the lone star where you work and is burning incense and candles to suppress everyone else from shining. Maybe it is that occult landlord or co-tenant that has stolen everyone else's glory in the compound and add them to hers. You should be very angry in your spirit as you have seen how wicked these powers are so pray these prayers like a mad prophet.

PRAYERS
1. **Every evil blanket covering my glory, catch fire and be roasted to ashes.**
2. **Every evil authority covering my glory and threatening to cut off my feet, thunder of God locate and paralyze them now in Jesus name.**
3. **Every licking roof over my life, be repaired by the blood of Jesus.**
4. **Anti-glory powers, hear the word of the Lord, the time has come for me to shine, therefore release me and let me go, in the name of Jesus.**
5. **O Lord God, arise and clothe my nakedness with your glory.**
6. **Every arrow of shame and disgrace fired into my destiny, jump out, and backfire.**
7. **I reject evil exchange and evil transfer. They are not my portion in the name of Jesus.**
8. **Every satanic exchange of my glory and virtues, be reversed by the power in the blood of a Jesus.**
9. **Every strongman that has vowed that over their dead body will I prosper, it is now time for me to prosper, therefore fall down and die.**
10. **Every evil umbrella covering my head, catch fire.**
11. **Every anti-glory dream, be cancelled by the blood of Jesus.**
12. **Blood of Jesus repair my vandalized glory in the name of Jesus.**

Witchcraft Powers

"There shall not be found among you any one that maketh his son or his daughter to pass through the fire, or that useth divination, or an observer of times, or an enchanter, or a witch. Or a charmer, or a consulter with familiar spirits, or a wizard, or a necromancer. For all that do these things are an abomination unto the Lord: and because of these abominations the Lord thy God doth drive them out from before thee." Deuteronomy18:10-12.

These are powers that manipulate your life and seek to use their diabolical powers to change God's plans and purpose for your life. They do not want you to fulfill your divine destiny.

There are various types of witchcraft. **Deuteronomy 18:10-12.** They include household witchcraft which is witchcraft that is perpetuated by the members of your own immediate family. This includes polygamous witchcraft which originates from a man having multiple wives at the same time.

There is marine witchcraft which is witchcraft from the waters. It fuels the rage of the waters against a person's life. Marine witchcraft powers are extremely wicked and their agents are everywhere, even in the church. They specialize in polluting and stealing from people.

There is anti-promotion witchcraft which prevents a person's life from progressing. It hates the advent of any new thing in such a life.

Environmental witchcraft is witchcraft activities originating from the environment where you school, live, work, attend church, and do business. Witchcraft altars and the pollution that comes from them can create loads of problems for you including poverty, madness, sickness, and death.

There is also envious witchcraft. These powers, spirits, and personalities are jealous of you and want what you have. They would go to any length to strip you of all that you have even if they have better things than you and leave you naked and stranded. You had better pursue, overtake and recover all your virtues, wealth, and goodness that they have stolen using the prayers below.

PRAYERS

1. Every damage done to my life by witchcraft powers be reversed by the blood of Jesus.

2. Every witchcraft twin stealing my blessings, fall down and die.

3. Every power, spirit, and personality contesting with me for my covering and my goodness, release them and die.

4. Every witchcraft altar and coven assigned against me catch fire.

5. I bind every follow, follow spirits destroying good things in my life.

6. Every spiritual warfare assigned against me in the heavenlies scatter.

7. Witchcraft eyes and gadget that are monitoring my life, catch fire.

8. Witchcraft brooms, mortars, cauldrons and other weapons working against my progress, be consumed by fire, in the name of Jesus.

9. Every witchcraft power and personality harassing my life, enough is enough, I cut off your hands and legs now with the sword of God.

10. Witchcraft garments militating against my glory, catch fire, roast.

11. Witchcraft chains, fetters, and padlocks militating against my progress, catch fire and burn to ashes.

12. Every power using witchcraft cobwebs to block my breakthroughs, fall down and die, in the name of Jesus.

13. Anti-promotion witchcraft, die.

14. Witchcraft networks militating against my progress, scatter by fire.

15. Every power summoning my spirit and calling my name for evil die.

16. My head reject every witchcraft control and manipulation.

17. I fire back every witchcraft arrow fired into my life.

18. Every evil hand preparing witchcraft calendar for me and turning the clock of my life backwards, be roasted with your calendar.

19. Witchcraft strongmen seating on my breakthroughs be unseated by fire.

20. I pursue, I overtake and I recover everything that witchcraft powers have stolen from me.

21. Thank you Lord for restoring everything that I have lost to witchcraft.

CHAPTER 9

CONSEQUENCES OF GOD DOING A NEW THING

Restoration

"And I will restore to you the years that the locust hath eaten, the cankerworm, and the caterpillar, and the palmerworm, my great army which I sent among you. And ye shall eat in plenty, and be satisfied, and praise the name of the LORD your God, that hath dealt wondrously with you: and my people shall never be ashamed." Joel 2:25-26

The manifestation of new things brings restoration in various areas of a person's life. This could be in the area of marriage, career, ministry, business, health, finance, and relationships. This restoration that results from God doing a new thing can manifest in various ways.

This restoration manifests when you get double for your shame and for all that you have lost. In the Bible, Job lost everything that He had. As a result his wife asked him to curse God and die. Even his friends judged him wrongly. But God who knows the heart knew the heart of this righteous man and restored everything to him in multiples. **Job 42:12-16.**

The restoration manifests when you recover all the wasted years in various areas of life. It manifests when you are accepted where you were previously rejected and celebrated where you were once mocked.

The restoration from God doing new things manifests when instead of demotion you are not only promoted but made the supervisor over your contemporaries. Daniel and his friends enjoyed this kind of promotion in Babylon. **Daniel 3:30.** The God of Daniel shall visit you today in Jesus name. I say the God of Shadrach, Meshach, and Abednego shall visit you today in Jesus name. That long awaited promotion is yours now.

The whole book of Ruth in the Bible is a story of God doing new things to bring about restoration in the lives of Ruth and her mother in law, Naomi. Ruth the Moabite and her sister in law, Orpah, were the widows of Naomi's sons. Unlike Orpah, Ruth decided to align herself with Jehovah, the God of Naomi, and His people. As a result of this decision, God, who is the God of new beginnings and new things manifested in her life and totally transformed it, bringing about massive restoration. Boaz, a kinsman redeemer to Ruth and a prototype of Christ, redeemed Ruth and married her. The baby from their union is a prototype of the new things that God does in our lives when we invite Him into our lives. These new things spring forth suddenly when we least expect or deserve them. It is truly by His grace alone. Today, I prophesy over your life, a new dawn, a new day, and new things in the name of Jesus.

The Lord God did a new thing also in the life of Naomi who had given up on life after she lost her husband and two young sons. Out of frustration, she made all sorts of negative confessions about her own life and changed her name from Naomi, meaning sweet, to "Mara" meaning bitter.

Unlike Naomi, who was busy tearing down her own life, Ruth was busy bringing positive changes to her life by giving herself a new name, the name of Jehovah, for she said, "Your God (Jehovah) shall be my God."

Ruth provided Naomi with a grandson, Obed who became the grandfather of King David and an ancestor of our Lord Jesus. **Ruth 4: 17.** In the end, there was so much restoration in both Ruth and Naomi's lives that their neighbors took notice of the new things that God was doing:

"And the women said unto Naomi, Blessed be the Lord, which hath not left thee this day without a kinsman, that his name may be famous in Israel. And he shall be unto thee a restorer of thy life, and a nourisher of thine old age: for thy daughter in law, which loveth thee, which is better to thee than seven sons, hath born him." Ruth 4:14-15.

Your restoration from the new things that God is doing manifests when new wonderful things cause you to forget the losses, pain, and sorrow of the past.

"Remember ye not the former things, neither consider the things of old." Isaiah 43:18.

"The sons also of them that afflicted thee shall come bending unto thee; and all they that despised thee shall bow themselves down at the soles of thy feet; and they shall call thee; The city of the LORD, The Zion of the Holy One of Israel. Whereas thou has been forsaken and hated, so that no man went through thee, I will make thee an eternal excellency, a joy of many generations." Isaiah 60:14-15.

Restoration manifests from God doing new things when joy is restored in the morning after the sorrow and tears of the night time:

**"Weeping may endure for a night, but joy cometh in the morning."
Psalm 30:5.**

This restoration manifests when the vehicle of your life is repaired and put back on the road by the Master Mechanic, Lord Jesus. It is when the broken wall of your life is rebuilt by the Master Craftsman, Lord Jesus.

"And they shall build the old wastes, they shall raise up the former desolations, and they shall repair the waste cities, the desolations of many generations." Isaiah 61:4.

PRAYERS
1. Every power speaking demotion into my destiny, die by fire.
2. I fire back every arrow of destiny demotion.
3. Where I have been rejected, I shall be celebrated.
4. Every vehicle of demotion prepared for me, catch fire and die.
5. Blood of Jesus repair the broken walls of my life.
6. Lord Jesus, You are the Master Mechanic, repair the vehicle of my destiny and put it back on the road again.
7. Any robber attacking my life, enough is enough, die now.
8. Power of restoration, locate my…. (Life, business, career, ministry).

Fruitfulness
"The LORD hath sworn by his right hand, and by the arm of his strength, Surely I will no more give thy corn to be meat for thine enemies; and the sons of the stranger shall not drink thy wine, for the which thou hast laboured: But they that have gathered it shall eat it, and praise the LORD; and they that have brought it together shall drink it in the courts of my holiness." Isaiah 62:8-9.

"And they shall build houses, and inhabit them; and they shall plant vineyards, and eat the fruit of them. They shall not build, and another inhabit; they shall not plant, and another eat: for as the days of a tree

are the days of my people, and mine elect shall long enjoy the work of their hands. They shall not labour in vain, nor bring forth for trouble; for they are the seed of the blessed of the LORD, and their offspring with them." Isaiah 65:21-24.

As the scripture above says, one of the results of God doing a new thing in your life is fruitfulness. This springs forth as the anti-harvest powers are paralyzed and the profitless hard work of the past is turned into fruitfulness and bountiful harvest. The wilderness turns into fruitful land. You get a reward for your labor and no longer work in vain. Make the following declaration loud and clear:

"I….. (Put your name here) will not labor in vain, in Jesus name."

Fruitfulness is when like Apostle Peter you have toiled all night long and caught nothing in life. Then out of the ordinary you hear the voice of the Lord Jesus telling you the exact spot to cast your net in the ocean of life. Then as you obey the Lord's voice you come out with such a huge catch of fish that your net is at the point of breaking. **(Luke 5:4-7; John 21:3-6).** That will be your portion this season in Jesus name. If you believe it, shout "Thank you Jesus" seven times for your bounty and then pray this prayer:

O God of Abraham, Isaac, and Jacob, make me fruitful in Jesus name.

Glory and Honor

"For the Lord is a sun and shield: the Lord will give grace and glory: no good thing will he withhold from them that walk uprightly." Psalm 84:11.

When the Lord does a new thing in your life, you are crowned with glory and honor. Your glory starts shining and people that previously mocked you start looking up to you. You move from strength to strength; from grace to grace; and from glory to glory. Anyone that stands in the way of your success becomes a stepping stone to your glory.

This was the case with Mordecai and his niece Esther who were Jewish slaves in Persia. God elevated Mordecai from gateman to prime minister and Esther to Queen, respectively. Haman, who opposed them was hung in the gallows that he prepared for Mordecai. Today every Haman planning your downfall shall die in your place in the name of Jesus.

Healing

"Beloved, I wish above all things that thou mayest prosper and be in health, even as thy soul prospereth." 3 John 1:2.

"Surely he hath borne our griefs, and carried our sorrows: yet we did esteem him stricken, smitten of God, and afflicted. But he was wounded for our transgressions, he was bruised for our iniquities: the chastisement of our peace was upon him; and with his stripes we are healed." Isaiah 53:3-5.

When the Lord does a new thing your health is restored. Healing is the children's meat. **Matthew 15:22-28.** Restoration brings healing of the body, soul, and spirit to the sick. Hezekiah was healed of his sickness when the God that does new things heard and answered his prayers. **2 Kings 20:6.**

Naaman, a general in the Syrian Army, had an encounter with the God that does new things and his leprous skin turned soft and beautiful like the skin of a baby. **2 Kings 5:13-15.**

Deliverance

"But upon mount Zion shall be deliverance, and there shall be holiness; and the house of Jacob shall possess their possessions." Obadiah 1:17.

The scripture from Obadiah above clearly tells us that with deliverance comes holiness. The result of these two things is that new things spring forth and the children of God are able to take possession of them. Even in the most difficult cases of captivity and oppression we are told that God is able to deliver to the uttermost. **Isaiah 49:24-26**

A classic example of God extraordinary ability to deliver is the case of the Demoniac. Not only was he delivered, but he turned into an evangelist overnight and went about telling people of the awesome things that Our Lord Jesus had done in his life. **Luke 8:39.**

Today you too will become an advertisement of God's power to deliver to the uttermost in the name of Jesus. Receive your deliverance in the name of Jesus.

Provision

When the Lord does new things, there is abundant provision. This happened in Samaria when there was a famine in the land. It was so severe that women were eating their children. **2 King 6:28-29.** The prophet Elisha stepped into the situation and prophesied a 24-hour miracle of abundance in Samaria. This prophesy came to pass exactly as the man of God had prophesied and there was abundance in the land. **2 King 7:1-20.** Pray the following prayer violently:

My divine provision, spring forth and locate me now! in Jesus name.

Your Story Changes

The story of your life changes when God does a new thing in your life. There is a turnaround and God uses the person's life to rewrite the history of his family. The story of Joseph is a classic example of God using a person to rewrite the person's family history. Overnight, he went from the prison to the palace and from being a prisoner to a being a prime minister. **Genesis 41:40-46.** His brothers who had despised him ended up bowing to him. The lives of members of his family were also preserved during the world wide famine as a result of Joseph's affluence and influence in Egypt.

The case of Abraham and Sarah is another. From being childless, not only did they become the parents of Isaac, the child of promise, but through Christ, they went on to become the father and mother of uncountable children like the stars of heaven. **Genesis 21:1-5, Genesis15:5-6.** We all as believers are Abraham's children through Christ.

Your story changes when stagnancy and backwardness in your life gives way to promotion and elevation. This ushers in new things through progress in marriage, academics, business, career, ministry, health and other areas of life.

PRAYER: O Lord, you that destroyed the prison garment of Joseph, arise and change my story today, in the name of Jesus.

Favor Pursues You

When God does a new thing, disfavor and hatred give way to divine favor.

"Surely the isles shall wait for me, and the ships of Tarshish first, to bring thy sons from far, their silver and their gold with them, unto the name of the LORD thy God, and to the Holy One of Israel, because he hath glorified thee. And the sons of strangers shall build up thy walls, and their kings shall minister unto thee: for in my wrath I smote thee, but in my favor have I had mercy on thee." Isaiah 60:9-10.

Esther was an orphan and a slave in a foreign country. The favor of God upon her life broke down all barriers and she was chosen out of many competitors to become the queen of the greatest king in her time. In the end, this opportunity enabled her to be used by God to deliver His people from destruction. **Esther 2:17-18.**

Joseph was sold into Egypt as a slave boy but favor pursued him everywhere he went. It eventually promoted him to being the prime minister of Egypt and a father to Pharaoh. **Genesis 45:8.**

PRAYERS

1. I prophesy that my appointed time, the season to favor me, is now.
2. Every mark of hatred and disfavor upon my life, be erased by the blood of Jesus.
3. By the power of the Holy Ghost, I connect to my helpers.
4. Every power killing or antagonizing my helpers, your time is up, die.
5. After the order of Esther, I declare by the blood of Jesus that I shall be chosen over all my competitors in the name of Jesus.
6. Blood of Jesus, Mercy of God, speak for me where I have no voice.
7. Power to be favored above all others fall upon me now.
8. O Lord, let your favor manifest in my life, in the name of Jesus.
9. Holy Ghost, arise by all the power by which you are known as God and connect me to my divine helpers.
10. Favor that brings reposition and recognition, fall upon my life.
15. I plug myself into the socket of divine favor, by the power in the blood of Jesus.
12. Any power anywhere assigned to help me, locate me by fire in the name of Jesus.

All Round Success

When God does a new thing in your life failure turns to success and defeat turns to victory. God did exactly that in the life of Hannah. **I Samuel 1 and 2**. Non achievement becomes history like it did in the life of Jabez. **1 Chronicle 4:10.** Where you had been failing you start exceling. Like Apostle Paul, uncommon and extraordinary testimonies become the order of the day. **Acts 9:1-7.** I pray that today marks the end of failure in your life in Jesus name. Make the following confessions very loud and clear:

CONFESSIONS
1. I am a success and not a failure in the mighty name of Jesus.
2. I am a victor and not a victim.
3. I am the first and not the last.
4. Every ancient strongman or strongwoman assigned to relocate me from the front to the back of the line, fall down and die now.
5. Where others have failed, I .... (Put your name here) shall succeed.
6. Every satanic road block erected against my breakthroughs collapse.
7. Every anti-success shoe upon my feet, catch fire and be roasted.
8. God by your mercy, arise and reposition me for success.
9. I receive the revelation that will put me at the right place at the right place.

CHAPTER 10

CONNECTING TO THE GOD OF NEW THINGS

We have spent the previous chapters of this book talking about the God of new things and the new things that He does in our lives. The question now is how do we connect to this God that does new things so that He can do the wonderful new things that we have learnt about in the first part of this book in our own lives?

There are certain things we should do if we want God to do new things in our lives. They will act as fertilizer for new things to spring forth in our lives. This season new things will indeed spring forth and germinate in every area of our lives in Jesus name. We will now look at some of these things.

Know Your God
"But the people that do know their God shall be strong, and do exploits." Daniel 11:32.

You should get to know the God that does new things and become His friend. This will give Him the opportunity to do wonders in your life and turn your life into a wonder. The scripture verse above tells us that those that know their God shall be strong and do exploits. **Daniel 11:32.** For this scripture to manifest in your life not only should you know Him, but you should remain plugged to His socket.

"Abide in me, and I in you. As the branch cannot bear fruit of itself, except it abide in the vine; no more can ye, except ye abide in me." John 15:4.

First of all you should confess all your sins, get be born again, and become a disciple of Jesus Christ. A disciple is one who follows the teachings, doctrines, and way of life of our Lord Jesus, in accordance with the scripture below:

"Go ye therefore, and teach all nations, baptizing them in the name of the Father, and of the Son, and of the Holy Ghost: Teaching them to

72

observe all things whatsoever I have commanded you." Mathew 28: 19-20.

We see that even though they were slaves in Babylon, a foreign country, Daniel and his Hebrew friends, Meshach, Shadrach, and Abednego, knew their God. They followed His teachings in their daily lives by refusing to eat food sacrificed to idols, or to bow before any idol.

"If it be so, our God whom we serve is able to deliver us from the burning fiery furnace, and he will deliver us out of thine hand, O king. But if not, be it known unto thee, O king, that we will not serve thy gods, nor worship the golden image which thou hast set up." Daniel 3:17-18.

This is why God continuously did new things in their lives because they knew Him.

You cannot expect God to do new things in your life when you have not taken the time to get to know Him and to become His child and friend. "Now" is the day of salvation the Bible says. **2 Corinthians 6:2.** Today, you can get saved and become His child. **(Please see the steps to salvation at the end of book).** You should repent of all known sins, turn away from them, and then ask Him to become the Lord of your life. After that, you should love and befriend Him and get to know Him better every day. **Psalm 91:14.** He is the greatest friend there is or can ever be. You are the sheep and He is the Shepherd who can meet all your needs. **John 10:27.** In Him indeed you should live, you move, and you have your very being. **Acts 17:28.**

Know and Apply the Word of God

The word of God is the manual that God has given His people to live by. Search the scriptures and learn the word of God as it pertains to your life and circumstances. Eat, chew, and digest the word of God daily. Meditate on and stand on the word for your new things to manifest.

"If ye abide in me, and my words abide in you, ye shall ask what ye will, and it shall be done unto you." John 15:7.

Forgive those that have offended you

"For if ye forgive men their trespasses, your heavenly Father will also forgive you: But if ye forgive not men their trespasses, neither will your Father forgive your trespasses." Matthew 6:14-15.

Refusing to forgive those that have offended you will hinder your prayers. God cannot forgive your sins if you refuse to forgive others that have offended you. **Matthew 18:35**. You cannot get new things from God without Him forgiving you your sins. Therefore, unwillingness to forgive others hinders prayers and keeps new things away. This is particularly true in the area of healing. Most people have received their healing **only** after they forgive those who hurt or treated them badly.

God is interested in our vertical relationship with Him as well as our horizontal relationship with one another. How we handle our horizontal relationships affects our relationship with Him. It is so important to God that our Lord Jesus said that if you know that a person is angry with you, you should go and settle the matter before bringing any offering to God. **Matthew 5:23-24.**

Have Overcoming Faith

"He (Abraham) staggered not at the promise of God through unbelief; but was strong in faith, giving glory to God." Romans 4:20.

You should put your trust totally in God and not in man. Believe that He will do for you all that He has promised you both in His written and rhema word. The bible requires us to live by faith and not by sight. **2 Corinthians 5:7.** Therefore, even when things do not appear to be so, believe and act as if they are so. **Romans 4:17.**

If your faith is not strong enough, ask the Lord, like the apostles did to increase your faith. Ask Him to give you that mustard seed of faith that you need to birth forth your new things. Pray that your faith will not fail you so that when God is birthing a new thing in your life, you do not come to birth and be unable to bring forth the new thing. **Isaiah 37:3.**

You should believe God's word to you, whether He give it directly to you or through His prophets, without doubting:

"Believe in the LORD your God, so shall ye be established; believe his prophets, so shall ye prosper." 2 Chronicles 20:20.

Your attitude should be "God said it, I believe it, and that settles it." Faith without works is dead. **James 2:26.** Now swing into action in the area of life that you are believing God to do a new thing for you. Put your faith to work and join the **Hebrew 11** Hall of Faith today.

Be Expectant

You should not only desire new things in your life but you should be expectant that God will do them. As you pray you should watch out for open doors of opportunity for the new things to manifest. The Prophet Elijah prayed for rain after three and a half years of drought. He was very expectant that rain would fall and kept asking his servant to go and see if the rain had started. A new thing did happen as abundance of rain sprung forth. His expectation was not cut off. **1 King 18:41-45.**

You too be expectant! Get that new jacket and that new brief case today for that new job that you have applied for. Get that new dress for that baby that you are expecting God to give to you this year. Get the shoes for that wedding that you believe is coming up this year. I prophesy over your life that as you do this by faith, your expectations shall not be cut off in the name of Jesus. God will grant you the desires of your heart in Jesus name!

Total Obedience

"Whatsoever he saith unto you, do it." John 2:5.

If you want God to do new things in your life, there should be total obedience to God and to the constituted authority that He has put over your life including pastors, parents, and secular government agencies. God considers partial obedience disobedience and procrastination is not allowed either. They both have a penchant for aborting new things.

"And Samuel said, Hath the LORD as great delight in burnt offerings and sacrifices, as in obeying the voice of the LORD? Behold, to obey is better than sacrifice, and to hearken than the fat of rams." 1 Samuel 15:22.

We should not be like King Saul or like Samson that allowed disobedience to abort the new things that God started in their lives. Not only did it abort good things but it also cut short their lives and destinies. King Saul lost his throne, his life, and his sons. **1 Samuel 31:6.** Samson lost his eyes and died with his enemies. **Judges 16:30.**

Total Trust and Dependence on God

Depend totally on God and not on other men or on your own strength. **Psalm 118:8-9.** Ensure that God is involved in everything that you do, even the minutest things. Recognize that He is the ultimate power and do not try to mix Him with strange and beggarly powers. **2 Kings 1:2-4.** Do not compound your problems by running like a headless chicken to sorcerers, voodoo men, psychics, and satanic prophets and priests for help. This is tantamount to lighting strange fires and they will consume you like they consumed the sons of Aaron who offered strange fire before God. **Numbers 3:4.**

The blessings from God make rich and have no sorrow added to them. **Proverbs 10:22.** On the other hand, any help that you get from Egypt has plenty of sorrow added to it and comes with a high price tag. Pray the following:

1. Father, I put my complete trust in you and you alone.
2. I will not go to my enemies for help in the name of Jesus.
3. I refuse to cooperate with my enemies, in the name of Jesus.

Pray Targeted Prayers

If you want the God that does new things to single you out for His blessings, then you should become a prayer addict. New things spring forth in the life of those who desperately seek God through prayers. They never cease praying. You should be well organized and pray targeted prayers as the enemy that you are fighting is very well organized.

Targeted prayers are bombarding, extended prayers that have been proven to be very effective in spiritual warfare. You pray them every day for a specified time. It requires that the correct prayers be applied to various situations that you face in life. **James 4:3.** Also the right prayers should be prayed at the right time for them to be effective. For example, you should pray against witchcraft at midnight when the witches hold their meeting.

Diligence and discipline is required in this very important area as we learn from the following scriptures:

"The effectual fervent prayer of a righteous man availeth much." James 5:17.

"When I cry unto thee, then shall mine enemies turn back: this I know; for God is for me." Psalm 56:9.

Prayers should be used to close all open doors through which the enemy can come in to kill, steal, and destroy the new things that God is doing in your life. You should also use the blood of Jesus and the fire of God to purge our life. Use it also to barricade your life and to stop further attacks.

Pray also against every enemy of the new things that God is doing in your life. For example, the spirit of Pisgah that operates at the edge of major breakthroughs to abort them. Pray against the strongman that has locked up your new things in his warehouse does not want you to have them. **Luke 11:21.** Your prayers will force him to release them to you.

PRAYERS

1. Every power assigned to be aborting new things in my life, fall down and die.

2. Every anti-breakthrough spirit working against my joy, die by fire.

Embrace Change

We should embrace change and let go of unprofitable traditions, if we want new things to manifest in our lives. All over the Bible we see that those that embraced change had new things to show for it. For example, the lepers of Samaria defied tradition and went to the camp of the Syrians to look for food rather than starve to death. **2 King 7:3-10.** Had they not defied tradition and done things differently there would have been no twenty-four hours miracle for them or the nation as a whole. Had Joseph not been sold into slavery, there would have been no opportunity to become a prime minister in Egypt or to preserve the lives of his family during the famine. **Genesis 41.** It was embracing change that led to an outstanding life of super achievements.

Be Courageous

"Be of good courage, and he shall strengthen your heart, all ye that hope in the LORD." Psalm 31:24.

All over the book of Joshua, we see God telling Joshua to be courageous as he led the Israelites to take over the land of Canaan. **Joshua 1:7, 9, 18.** If we want God to do new things in our lives, we have to be bold, courageous, and strong like Joshua and Caleb were. **Numbers 14:6-9.** As a result, they were the only men in their generation that partook of the new thing that God was doing. Everyone that left Egypt with them perished in the wilderness but they made it into Canaan land, the land of new things. Why? They were bold, strong, and willing to take risks because they knew that God was solidly behind them. They had full confidence in God. **Numbers 32:11-13.**

Be Thankful

"And the ransomed of the LORD shall return, and come to Zion with songs and everlasting joy upon their heads: they shall obtain joy and gladness, and sorrow and sighing shall flee away." Isaiah 35:10

We should cultivate a heart of thanksgiving if we want God to continue to do new things for us. The Bible records that our Lord Jesus healed ten lepers but only one of them came back to thank Him for his healing. The Lord appreciated this so much that He took him beyond the level of mere healing and made him completely whole. So this man was not only healed but totally restored in every area of his life. **Luke 17:11-19.**

As we too cultivate hearts of thanksgiving, God will go the extra mile to give us even more new things than we have asked for in various areas of our lives. So shall it be in Jesus name. Alleluia!

We should not only thank God for what He has done and is doing but also for what we believe that He will yet do in our lives. A heart of thanksgiving keeps away sorrow, discouragement, frustration, murmuring, and discontent. It also opens the flood gates of heaven to release your blessings to you!

Seek the Help of the Holy Spirit

In the Bible, we are clearly encouraged to ask the Holy Spirit for help:

"Likewise the Spirit also helpeth our infirmities: for we know not what we should pray for as we ought: but the Spirit itself maketh intercession for us with groanings which cannot be uttered." Romans 8:26.

"Then he answered and spake unto me, saying, This is the word of the LORD unto Zerubbabel, saying, Not by might, nor by power, but by my spirit, saith the LORD of hosts." Zechariah 4:5-7

The song writer reinforces the same need in the following song.

> I have no power of my own
> I have no power of my own
> Holy Spirit I come unto you
> Help me
> For I have no power of my own

It normally takes more than our human efforts to birth forth new things that originate from God. They are bigger than us and require God's involvement to come to pass. The Holy Spirit is the third person of the Godhead and the power that gets things done. We all need His help and should prayerfully ask for it.

At creation, He was the one that brooded over the earth when there was no form or shape. After that everything the Father spoke concerning the earth came into being. At the conception of our Lord Jesus, it was the Holy Spirit again that over shadowed Mary and she conceived and brought forth the baby Jesus without knowing any man. This same dynamite power of the Holy Spirit raised Jesus from the dead.

So we see that the Holy Spirit is a catalyst of new things. He has not changes. Even in our own lives He will do the same, in the Jesus name. As we seek His help, He will bring about positive changes and birth forth new things in our lives in Jesus name. He will catapult us to unimaginable heights in every area of our lives, in the mighty name of Jesus. Even so shall it be. Amen! Amen!! Amen!!!

Seek the Help of the Holy Spirit

> Likewise the Spirit also helpeth our infirmities: for we know not what we should pray for as we ought: but the Spirit itself maketh intercession for us with groanings which cannot be uttered. Romans 8:26.

> That I may be heard and quickened and up... ing. The book of the LORD... and Zerubbabel, saying... [this] might be oppressed... but to the princes... the LORD of hosts.   Zechariah 4:6.

...

Plant these words in your mind, and study them carefully:

        As I lived not of my own,
        That I began of no two
        Holy Spirit I enter into you
        Begotten me
        And I have an power of my own.

...

80

APPENDIX 1

STEPS TO SALVATION
(How to get born again)

1. Realize that all have sinned (Romans 3:23)

2. Repent of all your sins. (Acts 2:38)

3. Confess all your sins. (Acts 10:43)

4. Open the door of your heart so Jesus can come in. (Revelation 3:20).

5. Ask the Lord Jesus Christ to come into your heart as your personal Lord and Savior. (John 1:12)

6. Confess with your mouth that the Lord Jesus Christ is your Lord and Savior. (Romans 10:10)

7. Believe that you now have a new life in Christ Jesus and walk daily in that newness.

As you experience this newness in Christ and walk this new walk with Him, may you continuously hold His hands and walk with Him. May the Grace of our Lord Jesus Christ keep and preserve you until His coming in Jesus name.

APPENDIX 2

PRAYER SECTION

PLEASE TAKE THESE CHORUSES WITH ME:

1. The Man of Galilee
   You have done it before
   O yea O yea
   You will do it again

2. Pass me not O Gentle Savior
   Hear my humble cry
   While on others thou art calling
   Do not pass me by
   Chorus
   O Savior Savior hear my humble cry
   While on others thou art calling
   Do not pass me by

3. Do something new in my life
   Something new in my life
   Do something new in my life today
   Do something new in my life
   Something new in my life
   Do something new in my life today

O GOD ARISE AND DO NEW THINGS IN MY LIFE

1. God of new beginnings, arise and visit me today.
2. Where is the Lord God of Elijah? Arise and do new things in my life today.
3. O Lord, show me where to cast my net in the ocean of life, so that I can catch good fish.
4. Every evil attachment in my life, catch fire and be roasted to ashes.
5. Everything in my life stopping new things from manifesting, Hear the word of the Lord, come out and die.

6. Every power, personality and spirit militating against God's best for my life, somersault and die.

7. Every anti glory shoe upon my feet, catch fire and be roasted to ashes.

8. Blood of Jesus, blot out every evil hand writing working against the manifestation of new things in my life.

9. Holy Spirit, take the soap of heaven and the sponge of heaven and wash away every evil mark hindering me.

10. Every evil hand suppressing and oppressing my life, wither and burn to ashes.

11. Every Goliath oppressing my life, receive the stone of fire and die.

12. Every strongman sitting upon my new things be unseated by the fire of the Holy Ghost, somersault and die, in the name of Jesus.

13. Every opposition to the new thing that God is doing in my life, be dismantled by the power in the blood of Jesus.

14. Everything in me that is scaring God away from my life, give way now.

15. O Lord, show me areas of my life that I need change.

16. Every completed work of darkness done against my life, be reversed and be nullified by the blood of Jesus.

17. O Lord arise and give me new eyes and new ears.

18. God arise and give me a new heart, the heart of Jesus.

19. Lay your right hand on your head and pray this: Power to start afresh fall upon me.

20. Showers of blessings of the God that does new things fall upon every area of my life.

21. O God, who delights in surprising His children, visit me today.

22. Let new things begin to spring forth in every area of my life now (Marriage, career, ministry, business, health, etc.)

23. O Lord, open the flood gates of heaven and flood my life with new things.

OH LORD TAKE AWAY MY REPROACH

1. Every garment of reproach in my life, catch fire.

2. Every personality, power, or spirit assigned to take me by surprise die.

3. O God, arise and turn the reproach of those that despise me upon their own heads.

4. O God, expose and disgrace every witchcraft agent assigned to embarrass me.

5. My Father arise and waste every evil strongman in charge of my case.

6. Every evil bird flying for my sake, net of God, pull them down and let them be wasted.

7. Evil invaders assigned to infiltrate my spiritual life, be arrested now.

8. Let their evil assignments against me and my family fail and die.

9. Let their joy over my life be turned to sorrow, in the name of Jesus.

10. Instruments of bewitchment assigned against me, catch fire, be roasted.

11. Let every good prophetic utterance over my life begin to come to pass.

12. Season of opportunities and fulfillment open for me in Jesus name.

13. O God arise, and frustrate every power invading my spiritual life.

14. Doors of favor open for me now, in Jesus name.

15. Holy Ghost, angels of God, arise and pursue my divine helpers to me.

16. My God ordained spouse, I withdraw your peace and your joy, until you locate me by fire in Jesus name.

17. My God ordained spouse, I decree that you will not be able to sleep, eat, or function until you do what God has assigned for you to do in my life.

18. O God, arise, and cover those who seek my hurt with reproach and dishonor.

BLOOD OF JESUS WORK FOR ME

Song: (1) Barricade my life, blood of Jesus barricade my life. (2.) Blood of Jesus fight for me. (3.) There is power mighty in the blood

1. O God, arise and speak your mercy into every area of my life and destiny.

2. Blood of Jesus flow deep into every area of my life now and carry out deep cleansing, deliverance, and healing, in the name of Jesus.

3. Blood of Jesus, speak better things into my life now.

4. Blood of Jesus, dig deep into my foundation and uproot everything working against my life.

5. Blood of Jesus, cleanse me now, in the name Jesus.

6. Blood of Jesus, heal me where I need healing, deliver me where I need deliverance and transform me where I need transformation.

7. Blood of Jesus, flow into every area of my life and do a powerful work.

8. Blood of Jesus, repair every damage done to my destiny.

9. I put every area of my life in the pool blood of Jesus, for cleansing, healing, deliverance, and restoration, in the name of Jesus.

10. Blood of Jesus, set me free.

11. Blood of Jesus, arise and fight my battles for me.

12. I barricade my life with the blood of Jesus and the fire of God.

POWER AGAINST THE SPIRIT OF THE SPOILER
Scripture Reading: Judges 6: 1-24, Exodus 12:36

1. Every power assigned to spoil good things in my life die now.
2. Every power sowing garment of rejection into my life die now.
3. Everything done under the devils anointing to spoil my life be reversed by the blood of Jesus, in the name of Jesus.
4. O Lord, nullify the effect of every evil touch assigned to spoil my life.
5. O Lord, expose, disgrace, arrest, and paralyze all wicked spirits that are against my settling down in life, in Jesus name.
6. Every injury and damage done to my destiny be healed by the blood of Jesus
7. Spoiler spirits of my father's house, die now.
8. Spoiler spirits of my mother's house, die now.
9. Spoiler spirits in my environment, scatter by fire now.
10. Evil hands troubling my destiny, wither and catch fire of Jesus.

VICTORY OVER ANTI-HARVEST POWERS

1. Every anti-harvest power assigned to swallow up my harvest, you are a failure, die.
2. I will not sow and another reap, and I will not reap and be unable to enjoy it.
3. I will not build and another inhabit in the mighty name of Jesus.
4. Spirit of……. (Pick in the under list) I am not your candidate, die.

(a.) Profitless hard-work (b.) the spoiler (c.) the emptier

5. Every spirit of the emptier assigned against my life, die now.
6. Powers assigned to devour my harvest, fall down and die.
7. O Lord, restore all that anti-harvest powers have destroyed in my life.

PARALYZING MONITORING POWERS

1. Every follow, follow spirit following me about to destroy good things in my life, die, in the name of Jesus.

2. Monitoring gadgets assigned against my life break to irreparable pieces.

3. Every evil bird flying against my destiny, die now.

4. I destroy everything that is representing me in the demonic world.

5. I release blindness and confusion on evil powers monitoring my life.

6. Ancestral monitors assigned against me life, catch fire and be roasted.

7. Every evil eye monitoring my life for attacks, receive fire and be blinded.

8. Wicked powers monitoring my life, fall down and die, in Jesus name.

9. I bind and cast out every ladder of darkness, in the name of Jesus.

10. All those circulating my name for evil, paralyzed and be disgraced.

11. I cut off the hands and legs of every man or woman walking about for my sake.

12. Every monitoring and surveillance gadgets that are being used against me fall into the bottomless pit and be rendered useless.

POWER AGAINST SPIRITUAL THIEVES

Scripture: John 10:10

Song: So I go back to the enemy's camp and I take back what he stole from me.

1. I bind and render impotent every satanic door keeper and gateman.

2. I bind and render impotent every strongman and his strong-room harboring my blessings.

3. I withdraw every mandate given to any thief to steal from me.

4. I decree by the power in the blood of Jesus that none shall steal from my land unchecked in the name of Jesus.

5. I command ever spiritual thief to release my stolen blessings.

6. Power to pursue overtake and recover fall upon me now.

7. I pursue, I overtake, and recover everything stolen from me by robbers.

8. Angels of the living God locate every evil competitor and retrieve everything that has been stolen from me.

9. By the power of the Holy Spirit I tear the mouth of the lion and I recover all that belongs to me in the name of Jesus.

10. O Lord, restore to me everything that spiritual thieves have stolen from me.

OVERCOMING ANTI-TESTIMONY POWERS

Song: My miracle, my miracle is already here

1. Power for breakthrough in ……. (Name the area) fall upon my life.
2. Powers opening evil books against me before my helpers die.
3. Every evil tongue speaking against my breakthroughs be cut off by fire.
4. Every power, spirit, and personality, saying to me "Sorry, try again next time," hear the word of the Lord, you are a liar. Die by fire.
5. Powers assigned against my glory die now in Jesus name.
6. Powers killing the opportunities and good things around me, whoever you are and wherever you are, die now.
7. Powers that have vowed that I will not enter my Canaan Land, die now.
8. By fire, by force, I enter my Canaan Land now.
9. Strongman of my father's house saying no to my ……breakthrough, fall down and die.
10. Every padlock of darkness assigned against my progress, break.
11. Every power saying no to my testimonies, die.
12. You my breakthroughs, wherever you are, jump out and locate me.
13. My testimony, appear by fire, in the name of Jesus.
14. No weapon fashioned against me shall prosper in the name of Jesus.
15. Every power waiting to puncture and abort my testimony, die now.
16. Every battle at the edge of my breakthrough, die, in Jesus name.
17. Every breakthrough that I have received in my dreams manifest by fire.
18. I smash to pieces every demonic mirror monitoring my life.
19. Every pollution to my ……… (Name the breakthrough) breakthrough be washed away by the blood of Jesus.
20. Evil expectation of my enemies concerning my life, boomerang.

DEFEATING EVIL SHADOWS FROM THE PAST

Song: When Jesus says yes, no power can say no.

1. Power of yesterday troubling my today, your time is up, die.
2. Every evil rope drawing me backwards, catch fire, and roast to ashes.
3. Evil shadow of my past, contesting against my goodness, release me and let me go, in the name of Jesus.
4. Mistakes and errors from the past assigned to arrest my glory today and tomorrow, clear away by the blood of Jesus.
5. The error of my past life contending with my joy and fulfillment now, what are you waiting for, die in Jesus name.

6. Any power from the pit of hell saying no to my breakthroughs, you are a liar, be paralyzed.

7. Every partner from any past relationship holding on to my glory and star, release it by fire, in the name of Jesus.

8. O Lord, turn the joy of the tormentors of my life to sadness

9. Evil hands from the past working against my joy, be cut off in Jesus name.

10. Every power, personality, and spirit from my past that is refusing to let me go and fulfill my God ordained destiny, release me and let me go, in the mighty name of Jesus. (*Repeat over* **"Release me, let me go."**)

I AM THE FIRST I WILL NOT BECOME THE LAST

1. Every ancient strongwoman repositioning me from the front to the back your time is up fall down and die in Jesus name.

2. Every power prolonging my journey to breakthroughs, die.

3. Every spirit of sluggishness and backwardness in my life, die.

4. I reject left over blessings, I reject slippery blessings.

5. Arrows of rejection and disappointment fired into my destiny, jump out and backfire.

6. I reject the second place. I take my number one place back in every area of my life, career, in marriage, in ministry, calling, academics, and business in Jesus name. (**Do not lump together. Pray them one by one.**)

7. After the order of Esther and Joseph, I claim divine favor in every area of my life.

8. I reject the spirit of the tail and I claim the spirit of the head.

9. I receive angelic transportation to where God wants me to be now.

10. O Lord catapult me to greatness as You did for Daniel in the land of Babylon.

11. I hold the blood of Jesus Christ against slippery blessings.

12. Every evil hand sowing slow progress and sluggishness into my life, wither by fire.

13. Every satanic hold up organized for my sake, scatter by thunder.

14. Thank you Lord for showering your favor upon my life.

ABOUT THE AUTHOR

Pastor Morayo Isi currently pastors in the United States of America. She is a teacher, healer, prophet, and intercessor. She has been teaching the word since 1993 and has been in full time ministry since 2009. She is heavily involved in the ministry of deliverance which she strongly believes is the heartbeat of the Almighty God for the world today. Her life and ministry testify of that. She conducts deliverance, healing, prophetic and other workshops around the world. Her ministry is accomplished by miracles, signs, and wonders and rests on two keynote scriptures, **Isaiah 61:1 and John 14:12**.

She is a prolific writer and writes in various forums including her own blogsite **www.deliverancewithmorayo.blogspot.com**. She is also available to help you write your story. She has written several books including, "Deliverance God's Heartbeat for Today," "One Step Ahead," and "Do it Right This Time." You can contact her at**: (281) 965-6727; email: royalhousepublishers@gmail.com.**